Somehow We Survive

Somehow We Survive

An Anthology of South African Writing

edited by Sterling Plumpp

illustrations by Dumile Feni

Thunder's Mouth Press • New York • Chicago

Copyright © 1982 by
Thunder's Mouth Press
All rights reserved
Published by Thunder's Mouth Press
242 W. 104th St. 5RW; New York, NY

Illustration by Dumile Feni
Book and Cover design by Ray Machura

Funded in part by grants from the
Illinois Arts Council and the
Coordinating Council of
Literary Magazines.

Library of Congress Cataloging in Publication Data
Main entry under title:

Somehow we survive.

1. South African literature (English)—20th century.
2. Blacks—South Africa—Literary collections.
3. South Africa—Race question—Literary collections.
I. Plumpp, Sterling, 1940-
PR9364.9.S6   820'.8'0968   81-23240
ISBN 0-938410-02-4   AACR2
ISBN 0-938410-01-6 (pbk.)

Dedicated to
Nelson Mandela
confined to imprisonment on
Robben Island for his
activities against Apartheid.
And to all those who
fought in the past,
are fighting today, and
will continue fighting
in the future
until their victory is won,
                    AMANDLA!

Contents

I would like to thank Michael Anania for planting the idea and supporting the editor for years; Dennis Brutus, Amelia House, Keorapetse Kgositsile, James Matthews, Jimi Matthews, and Melba Kgositsile for supplying contacts and providing sources from which to make selections; Dumile Feni for the fertilizer his art gave to the words selected; the editorial and design staff of Thunder's Mouth Press for patience; Neil Ortenberg for undertaking the idea as a publisher; Ray Machura for his talented design; Mongane Serote for providing me with materials which heightened my understanding of South African literature; David Bunn for providing Nortje's poems from his unpublished *Oxford Journal*; and Guild of Tutor Press International College for allowing me to use poems from *Black As I Am* by Zindzi Mandela and Peter Magubane (*Black As I Am* won first prize in the 1980 Janusz Korczak Literary Competition for the best book, in any language, for and about children, published in 1978 and 1979); And Anderson Thompson for the treasured photograph of Nelson Mandela.

Sterling Plumpp

Preface

by Keorapetse Kgositsile

SOUTH AFRICAN literature, in many African languages
with varying concerns of form and content, has a long
rich tradition which the colonialist plunderer/usurper of
our country has not been able to destroy. In this
country, the most powerful artistic reflection of social
reality in *song* (which is what poetry strives to be) has
been and consistently continues to be, in African
languages. Despite the insistence of white liberal patrons
who feel that if you are black and not writing in English,
you're not writing at all, there are many more writers—
poets, novelists, dramatists—in South Africa who write in
their native languages than those who write in English.

The contemporary South African poet is able to
draw from imaginative exploration of and reflection on a
long history of struggle and rich cultural activity. The
African people of South Africa, since the formation of
the African National Congress almost 70 years ago, have
fought many freedom battles, including civil disobed-
ience, strikes, protest marches, boycotts, petitions and
non-violent demonstrations. But in the face of racist
regimes who continued to rule our land by the gun, the
African National Congress established its military wing,
Umkhonto We Sizwe. This revolutionary movement
has drawn into its fold some of the most talented poets
writing in South Africa; the theme of their poetry is
clearly and unapologetically political.

The poems in this anthology, drawn from this body
of revolutionary song, are not muffled; they do not come
on like low whispers or whimpers from some corner of
national decay; they are not perverse word games. These
poets want to be heard very clearly from the frontlines of
the revolutionary movement; they are participants in the
struggle, in national and international realities, in the
affirmation of life as creative activity. This anthology

projects the suffering, the fury, the hopes and the
determination of the people of South Africa and their
poets in the ranks of the national liberation movement.
It is representative, not of a "school" of poetry, but of a
national mood. It is not exhaustive. There will be
many more.

Introduction

By Sterling Plumpp

There are many possible ways to choose to do an anthology
of South African literature. This one intends to present a
wide variety of South African writers whose work has a
vision of life committed to a larger space than the
bondage which blacks and other individuals find under
Apartheid. The writers chose to deal with a variety of
themes including loneliness, love, celebration, joy, despair,
determination, tenderness, and longing. Their tones range
from anger to irony, from humor to pain.

South African literature is an art form that is in the
process of becoming. Individual sensibilities are bursting
forth from centuries of economic exploitation and cultural
genocide to self-definition as a step towards human
fulfillment. Literature, as man's clearest mirror, most
faithful commentator on the trials he undergoes, is
nowhere more evident than in South Africa since 1948,
when under the implementation of Apartheid 87% of the
country was sectioned off for whites. Blacks were shoved
into nine separate "homelands" according to national
culture (Xhosas in the Transkei, Zulus in KwaZulu,
Pedis in Lebowa, etc.), and coloureds and Indians were
cramped into bleak settlements. Living under Apartheid
has forced blacks to react in a manner that has spurred the
birth of a new literature. Though Apartheid is but a
footnote in the long history of oppression against Africans
by whites, it is nevertheless the most inhumane and brutal
example of butchery since Hitler's Nazism. Resistance
against the policies of Apartheid has resulted in major
upheavals, such as the heightened activities of the 1950s
and early 1960s which culminated in the Sharpeville
massacre, and the banning of the African National
Congress, and other progressive movements. Other
significant incidents include the 1976 Soweto uprising,
and the growth and increasing power of black trade
unionism which caused strikes and forced changes in 1980.

This political activity within South Africa since 1948 can be viewed as a demarcation line from which to place generations of writers. Conditions within the society caused writers to take stands which led to exile or imprisonment.

This anthology is an exposition of mature South African voices as well as a presentation of emerging writers with considerable talent and sincere commitment. Some of the work reflects the clarity and commitment of *Umkhonto we Sizwe* (the military arm of ANC), particularly the poems by Victor Matlou, Baleka Kgositsile, Keorapetse Kgositsile, and Bheki Langa. Some of it probes individual and collective sensibility under attack by the corrosive hand of Apartheid. All of the work is honest and forceful. Nortje's *Oxford Journal* poems are taken from a private journal he kept and appear in print for the first time.

In *Somehow We Survive,* South Africans are shown surviving somehow under the barbarity of inhuman conditions. Their collective voice is determined to end the nightmare of Apartheid through whatever efforts necessary at whatever costs demanded in the "Year of the Spear."

Amandla!

The Story
of My Day

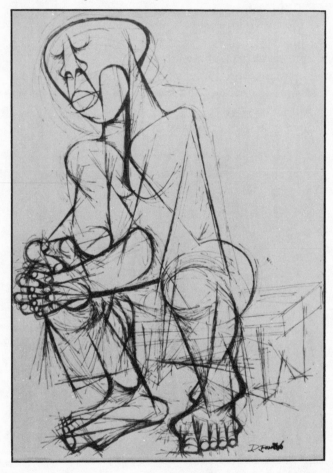

Prelude

Mongane Serote
from *Tsetlo*

When i take a pen,
my soul bursts to deface the paper
pus spills—
spreads
deforming a line into a figure that violates my love,
when i take a pen,
my crimson heart oozes into the ink,
dilutes it
spreads the gem of my life
makes the word i utter a gasp to the world,—
my mother, when i dance your eyes won't keep pace
look into my eyes,
there, the story of my day is told.

Saviour

Zindzi Mandela
from *Black As I Am*

An old woman standing
a young daughter opposite
both are waiting
in a wrinkled mind
      where are you Lord?
in a blossoming mind
      what are you Lord?
a white child running
a black child kneeling
both are young
in a polished mind
      a prayer tonight
in a deprived mind
      kneel all and sundry
an old man dying
a young son watching
both are pensive
in a dimming mind
      into your arms Lord
in a sorrowful mind
      release these chains

Dead Roots

Arthur Nortje

from *African Literature Today*

What I lose will have to be lost for life
& what I endeavour be tied into a concord
on this temporary isle,
I who wear
black flower in my buttonhole
hearing the demagogues
din in my ears
from the land of my fathers.
Invisibly reversed
by boom economies, quietly mutated
through golden ages,
there still live
my several lovers

    and I do not hate
    the sun still rising
    though nostalgic
    for that alien summer's
    cornucopia.

A minute's wavering in a winter bookshop
finds me turning tomorrow's pages
instead of deciding to buy the volume
suddenly thousands of miles away
climbing Table Mountain
& hoping a snake won't slither across my fingers.
I who have seen the maple & the snow
piled high in the moneyed northern streets
& came back to smell the rose among the spires
with a blessing for St. George
whether the fates will choose to twist
this clothed flesh into spirals of agony
round the entrenched & articulate bones
or whether the Paraclete
will intercede for such a one as I
dispersed Hotnot . . .

There were the stones wherewith
sparks were struck against the asphalt,
memory of my youth.
How they seem almost ancestral,
totems that inhabit dreams,
the carved faces now uncarvable:

> they are dead igneous, breaking rock
> on Robben Eiland,
> and I myself have lost
> sight of the long night fire.

AKN—11/70

Letter To Ipeleng On Her Birthday 1976

Keorapetse Kgositsile

But daddy I thought you was my *main man.*
Yes, mama, you *know* I am, said her father.
Then how come you won't tell me what the teacher said?
I'm sorry, Ipe, I was lying. Your teacher said
    nothing to me.
You know what, daddy? I think it's about time
    we stopped lying to each other.

What is it on your birthday
You want your main man to tell
Your peers who do not have the luxury
Of childhood or the tyranny of fear

How shall I say happy birthday
To you today when young blood flows
Down ghetto and small town streets
Where butcher savages practice their orgies
With jackboots, batons, bayonets and bullets

He was not much older than you
Who said: Father you cannot go to work
Today we will need some one to bury us
That, you must know and tell, is fidelity
To life not the slime of deathbound resignation
And your peers do not have the luxury
Of childhood or the tyranny of fear

He was not much older than you
Who said: Afrikaans, the language in a laager,
Was not the issue. *That* is a simple call to
LIBERATION IN OUR LIFETIME!
Not that it could ever be without pain
Not that that young skull smashed to pulp

Under fascist jackboot could not be your very own
But that the young blood that flows
Down those ghetto and small town streets
Can not be in vain

In our land fear is dead
The young are no longer young
The youth call to SPEAR-OF-OUR-NATION
To teach us the way and the means to
LIBERATION IN OUR LIFETIME
And you must possess and be possessed
By 'a thousand thundering voices
Which call you from the place of the sinking sun'

Because your peers do not have the luxury
Of childhood or the tyranny of fear
Remember this
There is no birth without blood
LIBERATION IN OUR LIFETIME
Is the only gateway to
Happy Birthday

(1975)

Waiting

Arthur Nortje
from *Dead Roots*

The isolation of exile is a gutted
warehouse at the back of pleasure streets:
the waterfront of limbo stretches panoramically—
night the beautifier lets the lights
dance across the wharf.
I peer through the skull's black windows
wondering what can credibly save me.
The poem trails across the ruined wall
a solitary snail, or phosphorescently
swims into vision like a fish
through a hole in the mind's foundation, acute
as a glittering nerve.

Origins trouble the voyager much, those roots
that have sipped the waters of another continent.
Africa is gigantic, one cannot begin
to know even the strange behaviour furthest
south in my xenophobic department.
Come back, come back mayibuye
cried the breakers of stone and cried the crowds
cried Mr. Kumalo before the withering fire
mayibuye Afrika

Now there is the loneliness of lost
beauties at Cabo de Esperancia, Table Mountain:
all the dead poets who sang of spring's
miraculous recrudescence in the sandscapes of Karoo
sang of thoughts that pierced like arrows, spoke
through the strangled throat of multi-humanity
bruised like a python in the maggot-fattening sun.

You with your face of pain, your touch of gaiety,
with eyes that could distil me any instant
have passed into some diary, some dead journal
now that the computer, the mechanical notion
obliterates sincerities.

The amplitude of sentiment has brought me no nearer
to anything affectionate,
new magnitude of thought has but betrayed
the lustre of your eyes.

You yourself have vacated the violent arena
for a northern life of semi-snow
under the Distant Early Warning System:
I suffer the radiation burns of silence.
It is not cosmic immensity or catastrophe
that terrifies me:
it is solitude that mutilates,
the night bulb that reveals ash on my sleeve.

1967

Midnight

Arthur Nortje
from *Dead Roots*

Tonight, precisely at that wall
my room's floor pauses in its walk,
throws up a gaze, observes the clock.
Bulb and brandy begin to talk.

Energy flows and sounds emerge,
but not from me—some alien source.
Beyond glass panels at my door
the darkness grins with utter force.

It creaked, the room's one empty chair:
devil or angel on my seat?
Outside my window, lamps bead blood
down on a tired waiting street.

The toilet gurgles by my ear,
sucks someone's paper down the drain.
Its chain keeps keeping vigilance
on odours of bowels, odours of pain.

Night after night I lie and wait
for sleep's return, but she, but she
is gripped in spastic fists of fear,
trembling at noises made by me.

South Africa, 1961

Sequence for South Africa

Dennis Brutus

from *South African Voices*

1.

Golden oaks and jacarandas
flowering:
exquisite images
to wrench my heart.

2.

Each day, each hour
is not painful,
exile is not amputation,
there is no bleeding wound
no torn flesh and severed nerves;
the secret is clamping down
holding the lid of awareness tight shut—
sealing in the acrid searing stench
that scalds the eyes,
swallows up the breath
and fires the brain in a wail—
until some thoughtless questioner
pries the sealed lid loose;
I can exclude awareness of exile
until someone calls me one.

3.

The agony returns;
after a crisis, delirium,
surcease and aftermath;
my heart knows an exhausted calm,
catharsis brings forgetfulness
but with recovery, resilience
the agony returns.

4.

At night
to put myself to sleep
I play alphabet games

but something reminds me of you
and I cry out
and am wakened.

5.
I have been bedded
in London and Paris
Amsterdam and Rotterdam,
in Munich and Frankfort
Warsaw and Rome—
and still my heart cries out for home!

6.
Exile
is the reproach
of beauty
in a foreign landscape,
vaguely familiar
because it echoes
remembered beauty.

Drink from my empty cup

Zindzi Mandela
from **Black As I Am**

Drink from my empty cup
and be proud
that nothing could quench your thirst

the reality
satisfied you
likewise
be hungry
crave for food
tremble at the sight of beer

kill
and feel free
then know
that you are so oppressed
you even laugh at yourself

Night Of Terror

Willie Adams

They came
with the early hour
of dawn.
Four unknown figures . . .
The knock on the door
at first soft
but urgent . . .
Then louder
and louder,
more urgent.
My wife was desperate,
in vain she tried
to awake me.
Later they shouted,
threatened to gate-crash.
But then . . .
still half asleep
I opened the door
to blink my sleepy
eyes onto four unknown faces.
Momentarily
I guessed their assignment
at three in the morning.
One of them produced
a pocketcard: Security Police.
My wife was hysterical
as I entered the white Volkswagen.
And I?
I questioned myself.
What at this early hour.
Couldn't they wait until daytime . . .
And I cursed
through my teeth.
What will happen
to my wife, my children?
And Beth—she's so small,

and tomorrow
when the neighbours ask
all these questions,
will my wife be able to answer-
Because of small things
such as your own ideas
you will be kidnapped
and driven away at dawn.

My Sister

Keorapetse Kgositsile

I could not come to see
What remained of you
Even if I had dared
I couldn't whiskey my way out of your eye
Any more than I could jump out of my skin
Even on the sixth day
After that treacherous Saturday
That whisked you away from us
I could not come to see
What remained of you

Your spectre patrols my restless moments
When I know I should be slitting fascist throats
Or poeting your determined purpose
But I bounce to impotence like a cheque
Foreign to you in your fashioning our future
I could not even whiskey my way out of your eye
Any more than I could jump out of my skin

Not that it would have made a difference
Had your hasty death on the Morogoro Road been foretold
That was what you had to do
Clearly as a philosophical choice
A meeting though at most of them
There is not much more than platitude or pretension
Clothes for the children though this day
Most remain as naked as their young souls

So now you are gone
You had to take a final road
Not chosen by you
And finally I came
And I looked
And I was chilled to numbness
A mouth full of cottonwool
Where your weighted smile used to be

Body all shrouded and deathly still
No missile from your tongue or eye
Which always demanded what and why
Later when I wished for rain
To come smother my impotent tears
Baba said
Only the pillow knows the tears of man

Now like my sister's embrace
Across the treacherous waters and centuries
I want to put my mouth on paper
The poet in me wants to carve
A monument in song
A simple song
Stronger than any granite wall
A song that says
Kate Molale is the people

But the poem won't come

The Blues Is You In Me

Sidney Sepamla
from *The Blues Is You In Me*

When my heart pulsates a rhythm
off-beat with God's own scintillating pace
and I can trace only those thoughts
that mar the goodness of living with you
then I know I've got the blues for howling

> yeah I've been howling
> clouds have been muffling
> and the rain has come
> and washed away
> these blues of mine

> the blues is you in me

I want to say it louder now
I want to holler my thoughts now
for I never knew the blues until I met you

> the blues is you in me

the blues is the clicks of my tongue
agitated by the death I live

the blues is my father's squeals
every Friday in a week

> the blues is you in me
> I never knew the blues until I met you

the blues is the screeches of the censor's pen
as he scribbles lamentations on my sensitized pad

the blues is the shadow of a cop
dancing the Immortality Act jitterbug

the blues in the Group Areas Act and all its jive

the blues is the Bantu Education Act and its improvisations

    the blues is you in me
    I never knew the blues until I met you

the blues is people huddled on a bench
eating of their own thoughts

the blues is those many words said to repair
yesterdays felled again and again by today's promises

the blues is the long shadow I count
measured by moments dragging the sun

the blues is the ratting of my brother
for opportunities he gets which he ought to have had

    the blues is you in me
    I never knew the blues until I met you

I want to holler the how-long blues
because we are the blues people all
the whiteman bemoaning his burden
the blackman offloading the yoke

    the blues is you in me
    I never knew the blues until I met you

Carnival at New Years

Julian deWette

The blackface crouches stealthily to frighten
onlookers; dust flattens underfoot
to mad frets of banjo strumming
and brown carnival players crumple satins
in sunbursts
sputtering through fire and vapours of dry ice.
A brown hand tangos, racing the dance:
an unchallenged southeaster
that dries faces and viscera to tautness,
breeds kestrels to mimic extinct bird voices
calling the dance in shoes
shod tight against the upper arch and heel.

Concertinas and brass wrestle strange songs
and Africa catches in the throat. Cape Town breaks
into mulatto dance,
contained, but unchecked
against breezes from another continent—
men partnering strange men
playing whiteface now, under combed coif.
The thrashing carnival tears up the tar-caked Heerengracht
exposing cobbles that once struck fire
under flint hooves. A distant energy unfolds
baring brown bodies to austereness;
rushed faces pant under heavy cosmetic.

Staffrider

Matime Papane
from *Staffrider*

I sleep
  In my box
  Away from pass-men
  But a knock
  Comes at my window
  Seeking my soul
  For a permit
  For a pass

Guns and bullets
  They barrel
  And brim
  On my side
  Of the cities
  I've built :
  They want my soul,
  My trespass.
  Right here
  I've laboured,
  Right here
  I'll be shot
  I am black

Note To Khatija

Essop Patel
from *Staffrider*

a union of stars engaged
in a silent conspiracy
with the urban darkness,
unobtrusively
life and death playing
a game of dice
danger
d
  a
  n
  c
   i
  n
  g
in a shebeen.
under the street lamp
an inebriated tramp
s
 h
  a
   d
    o
     w
       o   g
     b x n
       i
with a black alley cat . . .
tonight
baragwanath is breathing
like a sedated babe
in the arms
of soweto

Pimville Station

Sidney Sepamla
from *Hurry Up To It!*

On the one side
stood a ticket office
two poles overlooking it
one bringing light
the other a link with the world outside
both symbols of its higher status in the surroundings
Under the same roof
was a fish and chips shop
too busy frying to watch its smell
Behind it
was a sulky pair of toilets
The whole sight
was like a pregnant cockroach waiting expectantly

On the other side
languished
a ramshackle general dealer's
too old to care for its looks

The two sides were linked by a steel bridge
crouched over the single-track line
quizzically
like a hunchback resting elbows on a table

The platform looked like a street pavement
raised
waist-high
This was Pimville Station

As hundreds of passengers
jostled and scurried out of the fenced-in station yard
I came to understand the scene
on Noah's Ark
the day after the floods

The railway policeman on the beat
stood out in the crowd

like a lighthouse
he was always blowing hot and cold
to be at a pitch for arresting anyone

On and around the station
business was brisk:
peanut vendors
thugs frisking fellow-travellers
women roasting mealie cobs
and a herbalist brooding over a dry root

Each morning
before the eastern wink
could peek
into chinks of corrugated iron roofs
I would hear blinking in my sleep
a rumbling
as of agitated steel hoofs
the clank and clatter of rolling wheels
grousing about carriages
swaying under strain

Sometimes I heard
crammed passengers
chatter and grumble above others
bemoaning
increased house rents
early morning house raids
and the sordid drunkenness of their neighbours

So many times have I thought
about the defiant stance
of a railway station in a Location

my very first experience of
what is permissively called:
separate and equal amenities!

Leave Me Alone

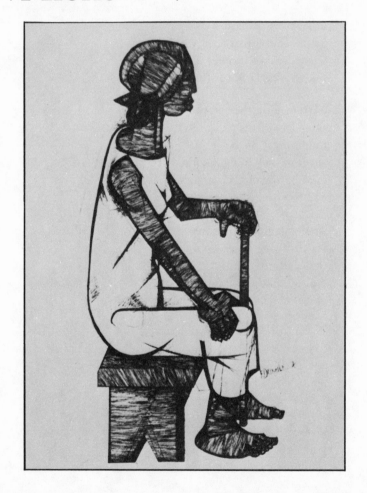

I Share the Pain Of My Black Brother

James Matthews
from *Cry Rage*

I share the pain of my black brother
and a mother in a Harlem ghetto
with that of a soul brother in Notting Hill
as I am moved from the land I own
because of the colour of my skin

Our pain has linked us
from Manenberg to Soweto
to the land of the not so free
and britannia across the sea

My black brother's cross his colour
the pages of his passbook the nails
that skewer his flesh
the towns of Alabama filled
with groves of ebony crosses
and the streets of liberty our calvary

Now our pain unites us
into burning brands of rage
that will melt our fetters
and sear the flesh of the mockers
of our blackness and our heritage

Heaven Is Not Closed

Bessie Head
from *Forced Landing*

All her life Galethebege earnestly believed that her whole heart ought to be devoted to God, yet one catastrophe after another occurred to swerve her from this path.

It was only in the last five years of her life, after her husband Ralokae had died, that she was able to devote her whole mind to her calling. Then, all her pent-up and suppressed love for God burst forth and she talked only of Him day and night— so her grandchildren, solemnly and with deep awe, informed the mourners at her funeral. And all the mourners present at her hour of passing were utterly convinced that they had watched a profound and holy event.

They talked about it for days afterwards.

Galethebege was well over ninety when she died and not at all afflicted by crippling ailments like most of the aged. In fact, only two days before her death she had complained to her grandchildren of a sudden fever and a lameness in her legs and she remained in bed.

A quiet and thoughtful mood fell upon her. On the morning of the second day she had abruptly demanded that all the relatives be summoned.

'My hour has come,' she said, with lofty dignity.

No one quite believed it, because that whole morning she sat bolt upright in bed and talked to all who had gathered about God, whom she loved with her whole heart.

Then, exactly at noon, she announced once more that her hour had indeed come and lay down peacefully like one about to take a short nap. Her last words were:

'I shall rest now because I believe in God.'

Then, a terrible silence filled the hut and seemed to paralyze the mourners because they all remained immobile for some time; each person present cried quietly, as not one of them had witnessed such a magnificent death before.

They only stirred when the old man, Modise, suddenly observed, with great practicality, that Galethebege was not in the correct position for death. She lay on her side with her right arm thrust out above her head.

She ought to be turned over on her back, with her hands crossed over her chest, he said. A smile flickered over the old man's face as he said this, as though it was just like Galethebege to make a miscalculation.

Why, she knew the hour of her death and everything, then forgot at the last minute the correct sleeping posture for the coffin. And later that evening, as he sat with his children near the out-door fire for the evening meal, a smile again flickered over his face.

'I am of a mind to think that Galethebege was praying for forgiveness for her sins this morning,' he said slowly. 'It must have been a sin for her marry to Ralokae. He was an unbeliever to the day of his death . . .'

A gust of astonished laughter shook his family out of the solemn mood of mourning that had fallen upon them and they all turned eagerly towards their grandfather, sensing that he had a story to tell.

'As you all know,' the old man said, wisely. 'Ralokae was my brother. But none of you present knows the story of Galethebege's life, as I know it . . .'

And as the flickering firelight lit up their faces, he told the following story: 'I was never like Ralokae, an unbeliever. But that man, my brother, draws out my heart. He liked to say that we as a tribe would fall into great difficulties if we forgot our own customs and laws. Today, his words seem true. There is thieving and adultery going on such as was not possible under Setswana law.'

In those days when they were young, said the old man, Modise, it had become the fashion for all Black people to embrace the Gospel. For some it was the mark of whether they were 'civilized' or not. For some, like Galethebege, it was their whole life.

Anyone with eyes to see would have known that Galethebege had been born good under any custom, whether Setswana or Christian, she would still have been good. It was this natural goodness of heart that made her so eagerly pursue the word of the Gospel. There was a look on her face, absent, abstracted, as though she needed to share the final secret of life with God, who would understand all things. So she was always on her way to church, and in hours of leisure in life would have gone on in this quiet and worshipful way, had not a sudden catastrophe occurred in the yard of Ralokae.

Ralokae had been married for nearly a year when his young wife died in childbirth. She died when the crops of the season were being harvested, and for a year Ralokae imposed on himself the traditional restraints and disciplines of *boswagadi* or mourning for the deceased.

A year later, again at the harvest time, he underwent the cleansing ceremony demanded by custom and could once more resume the normal life of a man. It was the unexpectedness of the tragic event and the discipline imposed on him that made Ralokae take note of the life of Galethebege.

She lived just three yards away from his own yard and formerly he had barely taken note of her existence; it was too quiet and orderly. But during that year of mourning it delighted him to hear that gentle and earnest voice of Galethebege inform him that such tragedies 'were the will of God.'

As soon as he could, he began courting her. He was young and impatient to be married again and no one could bring back the dead. So a few days after the cleansing ceremony, he made his intentions very clear to her.

'Let us two get together,' he said. 'I am pleased by all your ways.' Galethebege was at the same time startled, pleased, and hesitant. She was hesitant because it was well known that Ralokae was an unbeliever; he had not once set foot in church. So she looked at him, begging an apology, and mentioned the matter which was foremost in her mind.

'Ralokae,' she said, uncertainly, 'I have set God always before me,' implying by that statement that perhaps he was seeking a Christian life too, like her own. But he only looked at her in a strange way and said nothing. This matter was to stand like a fearful sword between them but he had set his mind on winning Galethebege as his wife. That was all he was certain of. He would turn up in her yard day after day.

'Hello, girl friend,' he'd greet her, enchantingly.

He always wore a black beret perched at a jaunty angle on his head, and his walk and manner were gay and jaunty too. He was so exciting as a man that he threw her whole life into turmoil. It was the first time love had come her way and it made the blood pound fiercely through her whole body till she could feel its very throbbing at the tips of her fingers.

It turned her thoughts from God a bit to this new magic life was offering her. The day she agreed to be his wife, that sword quivered like a fearful thing between them. Ralokae said quietly and finally: 'I took my first wife according to the old customs. I am going to take my second wife according to old customs too.'

He could see the protest on her face. She wanted to be married in church according to the Christian custom but he also had his own protest to make. The God might be all right, he explained. But there was something wrong with the people who had brought the word of the Gospel to the land. Their love was enslaving Black people and he could not stand it.

That was why he was without belief. It was the people he did not trust. They were full of tricks. They were a people who, at the sight of a Black man, pointed a finger in the air, looked away into the distance and said, impatiently: 'Boy! Will you carry this! Boy! Will you fetch this!'

They had brought a new order of things into the land and they made the people cry for love. One never had to cry for love in the customary way of life. Respect was just there for the people all the time. That was why he rejected all things foreign.

What did a woman do with a man like that who knew his own mind? She either loved him or she was mad. From that day on Galethebege knew what she would do. She would do all that Ralokae commanded, as a good wife should.

But her former life was like a drug .Her footsteps were too accustomed to wearing down the foot-path to the church, so they carried her to the home of the missionary which stood just under its shadow.

The missionary was a short, anonymous-looking man who wore glasses. He had been the resident missionary for some time and, like all his fellows, he did not particularly like the people. He always complained to his kind that they were terrible beggars and rather stupid. So when he opened the door and saw Galethebege there his expression with its raised eyebrows clearly said: 'Well what do you want now?'

'I am to be married, sir,' Galethebege said, politely, after the exchange of greetings.

The missionary smiled: 'Well come in, my dear. Let us talk about the arrangements.'

He stared at her with polite, professional interest. She was a complete nonentity, a part of the vague black blur which was his congregation—oh, they noticed chiefs and people like that, but not the silent mass of the humble and lowly who had an almost weird capacity to creep quietly through life. Her next words brought her sharply into focus.

'The man I am to marry, sir, does not wish to be married in the Christian way. He will only marry under Setswana custom,' she said softly.

They always knew the superficial stories about 'heathen customs'; an expression of disgust crept into his face—sexual malpractices had been associated with the traditional marriage ceremony and (shudder!) they draped the stinking intestinal bag of the ox around the necks.

'That we cannot allow!' he said sharply. 'Tell him to come and marry the Christian way.'

Galethebege started trembling all over. She looked at the missionary in alarm. Ralokae would never agree to this. Her intention in approaching the missionary was to acquire his blessing for the marriage, as though a compromise of tenderness could be made between the two traditions opposed to each other.

She trembled because it was beyond her station in life to be involved in controversy and protest. The missionary noted the trembling and alarm and his tone softened a bit, but his next words were devastating.

'My dear,' he said, persuasively, 'Heaven is closed to the unbeliever . . .'

Galethebege stumbled home on faint legs. It never occurred to her to question such a miserable religion which terrified people with the fate of eternal damnation in hell-fire if they were 'heathens' or sinners. Only Ralokae seemed quite unperturbed by the fate that awaited him. He smiled when Galethebege relayed the words of the missionary to him.

'Girl friend,' he said, carelessly. 'You can choose what you like, Setswana custom or Christian custom. I have chosen to live my life by Setswana custom.'

Never once in her life had Galethebege's integrity been called into question. She wanted to make the point clear.

'What you mean, Ralokae,' she said firmly, 'is that I must choose you over my life with the church. I have a great love in my heart for you so I choose you. I shall tell the priest about this matter because his command is that I marry in the church.'

Even Galethebege was astounded by the harshness of the missionary's attitude. The catastrophe she never anticipated was that he abruptly excommunicated her from the church. She could no longer enter the church if she married under Setswana custom.

It was beyond her to reason that the missionary was the representative of both God and something evil, the mark of 'civilization.' It was unthinkable that an illiterate and ignorant man could display such contempt for the missionary's civilization. His rage and hatred were directed at Ralokae, but the only way in which he could inflict punishment was to banish Galethebege from the church. If it hurt anyone at all, it was only Galethebege.

The austere rituals of the church, the mass, the sermons, the intimate communication in prayer with God—all this had thrilled her heart deeply. But Ralokae was also representative of an ancient stream of holiness that people had lived with before any white man had set foot on the land, and it only needed a small protest to stir up loyalty for the old customs.

The old man, Modise, paused at this point in the telling of his tale, but his young listeners remained breathless and silent, eager for the conclusion.

'Today,' he continued, 'it is not a matter of debate because the young care neither way about religion. But in that day, the expulsion of Galethebege from the church was a matter of debate. It made the people of our village ward think.

'There was great indignation because both Galethebege and Ralokae were much respected in the community. People then wanted to know how it was that Ralokae, who was an unbeliever, could have heaven closed to him.

'A number of people, all the relatives who officiated at the wedding ceremony, then decided that if heaven was closed to Galethebege and Ralokae, it might as well be closed to them too, so they all no longer attended church.

'On the day of the wedding, we had all our own things.

Everyone knows the extent to which the cow was a part of the people's life and customs.

'We took our clothes from the cow and our food from the cow and it was the symbol of our wealth. So the cow was a holy thing in our lives. The elders then cut the intestinal bag of the cow in two, and one portion was placed around the neck of Galethebege and one portion around the neck of Ralokae to indicate the wealth and good luck they would find together in married life.

'Then the porridge and meat were dished up in our *mogopo* bowls which we had used from old times. There was much capering and ululating that day because Ralokae had honoured the old customs . . .'

A tender smile once more flickered over the old man's face.

'Galethebege could never forsake the custom in which she had been brought up. All through her married life she would find a corner in which to pray. Sometimes Ralokae would find her so and ask: 'What are you doing, Mother?' And she would reply, 'I am praying to the Christian God.'

The old man leaned forward and stirred the dying fire with a partially burnt-out log of wood. His listeners sighed, the way people do when they have heard a particularly good story. As they stared at the fire they found themselves debating the matter in their minds, as their elders had done forthy or fifty years ago. Was heaven really closed to the unbeliever, Ralokae?

Or had the Christian custom been so intolerant of Setswana custom that it could not bear the holiness of Setswana custom? Wasn't there a place in heaven too for Setswana custom? Then that gust of astonished laughter shook them again. Galethebege had been very well known in the village ward over the past five years for the supreme authority with which she talked about God. Perhaps her simple and good heart had been terrified that the doors of heaven were indeed closed on Ralokae and she had been trying to open them.

Native's Letter

Arthur Nortje
from *Lonely Against the Light*

Habitable planets are unknown or too
far away from us to be
of consequence. To be of
value to his homeland must the wanderer
not weep by northern waters, but love
his own bitter clay
roaming through the hard cities, tough
himself as coffin nails.

Harping on the nettles of his melancholy,
keening on the blue strings of the blood,
he will delve into mythologies perhaps
call up spirits through the night.

Or carry memories apocryphal
of Tshaka, Hendrik, Witbooi, Adam Kok,
of the Xhosa nation's dream
as he moonlights in another country:

but he shall also have
cycles of history
outnumbering the guns of supremacy.

Now and wherever he arrives
extending feelers into foreign scenes
exploring times and lives,
equally may he stand and laugh,
explode with a paper bag of poems,
burst upon a million televisions
with a face as in a Karsh photograph,
slave voluntarily in some siberia
to earn the salt of victory.

Darksome, whoever dies
in the malaise of my dear land

remember me at swim,
the moving waters spilling through my eyes:
and let no amnesia
attack at fire hour:
for some of us must storm the castles
some define the happening.

Toronto, May 1970

Speak to me of mushrooms

Dennis Brutus
from *GAR*

Speak to me of mushrooms
and mean aphrodisiacs
or nuclear clouds.
Speak to me of oysters
and mean pearls
or aphrodisiacs,
of dying
in the Elizabethan orgasmic sense
and the great relieving shuffle
of the burdensome flesh:
only speak to me
while I make music between your thighs
and let dear sorrowing tortured Yeats
rack himself in the shadows
beating upon a wall.
It is tenderness I need—
a great longing crying at the ends
of the tactile nerves
in glands and nipples,
queasily sliding in the groin:
Oh we are born to be aesthetes
to yield reluctant homage to a tree profile
poised and outlined against the lilac dusk
and all this tidal surge of lust
is surrogate for loneliness.
Where is my consolation? Where?
Sorrow with me in the bomb-drizzled skies of Vietnam
and twist with bruised hips on concrete
as my friends in prison:
Speak to me of mushrooms,
oysters,
while I make music
between your thighs.

Chimid: A Memorial

Keorapetse Kgositsile

Chimid my eye sprung out at the airport
Sprung out of the aeroplane window
To embrace you two years after Berlin
Berlin and Dresden
Dresden when we witnessed
The barbaric destruction of humanity
Screaming through rock and gaping wound
Of stone buildings bespeaking anguished memory

SOUTH AFRICA a poster
Boldly proclaimed in the hands
Of Erdene my Guide and Sister

Where is Chimid!
Anxiously I asked
Being no friend to casual disappointment
The Poet? . . . . Yes
He died some months ago

Chimid we lie to ourselves so much!
With admirable intent no doubt
We say
Death will not surprise us but
HE DIED . . .
And speech froze behind my tongue

If I said I felt pain
I would be lying to myself again
I was simply numbed
Even my possible tears
Froze behind my eyes

Chimid need I remind anyone
Who knows life
That death is treacherous
That death is a fascist monster
Who destroys without creating

An alternative you always desired
Who takes without giving
Who surprises us
As if he were not to be expected

Chimid Poet
Creator of manmaking words
Chimid Ulan-Bator Red Hero
Beacon of our future
We shall carve your monumental name
As we fight
For the progress and peace
You wrote and fought for
All over this planet

Awakening

Amelia House
from *Staffrider*

Into the fleapit. A collection of drunks, junkies, prostitutes, robbers—a gathering of human debris. Although trying to hide himself, the fat, little man in the corner was perhaps most noticeable of all. He clutched a satchel under one arm, while he tried to wipe the dirt off his neat, dark-blue, pin-striped suit. His round face and bald head shone although this belied the dullness he felt inside. Two women chatted loudly as they leaned against a side wall. Their hair had been freshly hot-combed for the evening's work, lips were made rounder and fuller with pillar-box red lipstick. Both smoked defiantly. Their "Evening-in-Paris" perfume would normally be offensively overpowering but here it was a welcomed smell. It penetrated the mixture of lingering dagga, sour wine and beer, sweat and urine. Two drunks lay, out cold, on the floor. A number of other regulars filled the pit. They were the night's take and would appear before the magistrate in the morning.

"Here's a teacher. Perhaps you can teach him something. They're the high and mighty, hey!" cackled the policeman.

'How's about a show then?' shouted one of the customers.

'Yea, Down, Mr. Library. Teach them to say "Please, my Basie!" Do it nicely on your knees.'

Eric had no will to argue.

'That's nice. Hands together. Hey you, join the show. You can piss all over this nice teacher.'

A tough looking young man stepped forward. Even in his complete abjection, Eric sensed that this scene had been staged before. The other actors were regulars in their roles. Eric realized he could only endure this by removing his mind from this terrible scene.

At the desk, the clerk for the night was going through Eric's belongings. He was a middle-aged man who had not progressed beyond sergeant. A kindly man who believed in giving the offenders a chance to mend their ways. When he joined the service, he believed he would be able to effect some change. He found Eric's name and address in his wallet. He recognized it as that of the postman on their beat.

'I thought he looked familiar. Those young policemen seem to belong to another breed. They would hate to see any offender go straight. They delight in crime, seek out crime or even create it. I wish I had the courage to speak out. I'm sure Eric Peterson is innocent. If I speak out now I will probably be dismissed and lose my pension.'

Sergeant de Vos had witnessed these scenes nightly but he had grown tired of crusading—tilting at windmills.

'If I call Mr. Peterson now, he will be able to fetch his son before midnight. Eric will then not have to appear in court. Strange though, I thought his son didn't smoke or drink. That family doesn't deserve the disgrace.'

Sergeant de Vos almost welcomed the commotion he heard from the cells. He could not risk the other policemen knowing of the phone call.

For Eric it had been another late evening. He had to attend lectures at the University after a day's teaching. He taught English and Science at the High School and was studying at night to complete his Bachelor's Degree in English and Economics. Every Wednesday evening he worked in the library until it closed half-past nine. He had to sprint to the stop to get the last bus down to the railway station. After a long day, he did not want to face a three mile walk.

Tonight the streets were deserted. He felt as if everybody had gone to shelter from a threatening storm.

'I seem to be the only one around tonight. I didn't see Dr. Jay in the library,' he chatted to the bus driver.

Normally a White driver might resent the over-friendliness

from a Coloured, but this driver had driven the Varsity bus so long that he knew most the students.

'Dr. Jay probably knew how to save his skin. Got away early. Agitator. They can give him a fancy title—Professor of African Studies—he's nothing but a damn Communist. I wouldn't be driving the bus if I didn't have to. It's the bread and butter for my family. Today was terrible.'

'What happened?'

'Where've you been? Everybody was warned to stay home because of the riots.'

'What riots?'

'Didn't you hear the radio? I suppose you were busy in the archives. You students spend time on Ancient History and don't know what's happening right now. That's education for you. I hope my children learn more useful things.'

'Who started the riots?'

'I was driving up the road when I saw the huge crowd of natives. They were like swarming locusts.'

'I suppose there were not more than fifty. Even the Blacks would be a crowd to you.'

'I mean hundreds. They were singing and shouting.'

'Singing is no crime.'

The driver ignored Eric's interruptions.

'A young boy led them. I won't be surprised if he isn't a Varsity student. Give those people a little education and they all become agitators. What does the native want with education?'

Eric did not want to hear a long tirade about the ungratefulness of the native, but he was anxious to find out the events of the day. He felt as if he had emerged from hibernation. He let the driver drone on.

'That young boy led the group from Langa all the way to Cape Town. That's easy twenty miles, I guess. They went to the Court House, Caledon Square, with some petition.'

'Lord knows they have enough to complain about,' muttered Eric.

'Their leader made a speech. He said they had no weapons. It was a peaceful demonstration. Any fool knows those *knobkieries* they walk with are powerful weapons.'

'Hardly a match for guns.'

'They demanded this, that and the other. The Commandant was clever though. He said he would speak to the leader if the crowd went away.'

'So the people once more fell for that old trick.'

'You know, those stupid people had to be shot at first before they would go away. I suppose the Commandant is still speaking to their leader.'

'You mean he was arrested,' Eric involuntarily commented.

'No. He was allowed to go in with his petition.' The driver pretended not to know the true nature of the interview. 'Those peaceful *Kaffirs* swarmed into a riot. Their swinging *kieries* caused much damage as locusts do to a crop. I'll be glad to be home. My wife must be worried. Emergency radio messages were broadcast. Warnings to clear the streets.'

'How many shots were fired by the police?'

The driver still ignored Eric's comments.

'The shopkeepers quickly bolted their stores. The *kieries* smashed windows and displays were looted. The damage was terrible.'

'How many were shot in the back?'

'Their leader's interview will be a long one.'

'They were betrayed if he was arrested. What else can we expect?'

'Why do you Coloureds at Varsity always side with the Natives?'

'We all belong to the Oppressed.'

'You all become Communists at that place. What can you expect—when even a Native is a Professor. Your parents want you to be decent. My children will not go up that mountain to that ivy-covered building—Communist breeding place. They'll go to Stellenbosch.'

Eric did not care to comment.

'At Stellenbosch they will know they are *Afrikaaners*.'

The driver had started on one of his favourite topics.

'There are too many Jews at his place. The Ikies try to be nice to everybody. That doesn't work. We can't all be bosses. As we *Afrikaaners* say, if I'm boss and you're boss, who will grease the wagon wheels?'

Eric retreated to his reading.

He could not concentrate. He though of Dr. Jay. They usually rode the bus together. Had he heard of the riots? Dr. Jay lived in Langa.

As the bus reached the railway station, Eric recalled the driver's account. The police were out in force. With truncheons guns at the ready, they were prepared for an invasion.

Just as Eric got to the station, he saw Dr. Jay get out of a car.

Dr. Jay was immediately pounced on.

'Where is your pass, *Kaffir?*, the policeman demanded.

Dr. Jay fumbled untidily in the pockets of his neat dark-blue pinstriped suit. His satchel was pulled out of his hand, the contents strewn on the ground.

'Quick. Your pass!'

'That's Professor Jay. How can you treat him like that?' Eric blurted.

'Shut up. Do you want to be arrested for obstructing justice?'

Dr. Jay attempted to retrieve his books and papers. He joined them as he was knocked down.

'You Communists teach decent Kaffirs to riot. You're the cause of the trouble we had today.'

Eric's train arrived. How could he erase the picture of Dr. Jay on the pavement amid his books? He could not concentrate on his reading. Usually he buried himself in a book for the half-hour ride. Tonight he stared blankly out the window at the dark mountain. Table Mountain seemed to cast a shadow over the whole world tonight.

'Good evening, Teach. Gotta a cigarette for me?'

Eric continued to stare.

'I'm asking nicely, Teach. All I want is a cigarette,' he nudged Eric.

'Oh, yes. I don't smoke, but here you can buy some.'

The next moment Eric had knuckle-dusters under his nose. The *skolly* stood over him.

'I'm the gentle fellow. I do like your watch. I'm not violent. I annex property peacefully.'

Eric wanted to protest. This was the first watch he ever owned—bought with his first pay cheque. He handed over his watch. He knew better than to argue. Two other *skollies* were watching.

'Tell us the time on your Big Ben.'

'He doesn't know how to tell time,' teased one of the onlookers.

The one had put on the watch but he still stood over Eric as if deciding what next to annex.

'Hey, pal, leave the teacher alone,' one whined. 'I know his Dad. Used to teach me Sunday School.'

Even Eric almost joined in the laughter that was evoked by the idea that any of them had attended Sunday School.

Eric offered no comment. He knew the rules. If he tried to defend himself, he might be beaten up, even stripped. He did not want to relive that experience. That had happened to him in College.

Although the *skollies* terrified Eric, he could not help feeling a sadness at the waste of their lives. They could be making a positive contribution to their community. A few of the *skollies* came from good homes, but they allowed themselves to be ruled by the 'tough leaders.' Some of them even had some schooling. They bolstered their manhood with *dagga* and knife-fights. None of them had regular jobs, so they preyed mainly on the 'decent people' in their own community. They wore pants cut off below the knees, caps with peaks to side or back. They walked with a special skip-step—both hands in pants pockets stuck out to the sides. They usually had gang affiliations and often congregated on street corners. There they rolled dice, sang and smoked *dagga*. Although the community feared them, their ready wit and sense of humour were admired and copied. ,

'Kenilworth. Kenilw-o-r-th . . . Wynberg . . . next stop!' the conductor shouted.

Home was near. He could almost smell the good food. What a long day.

He was out and headed for the bridge before the train had

completely stopped. Home. Then he remembered that the bridge was now 'Whites Only.' He doubled back to the other end of the platform. He had to use the subway. On this station the policemen were also well represented. Their absence would have surprised him. Only two other passengers had got off. Here too the people seemed in hiding. He felt the need to get home quickly.

He ran down the steps and jumped the last two. Instead of landing on his feet, he found himself carried a few paces by two policemen.

'Where do you think you're going? You're not supposed to be on the streets.'

'*Ja*, everybody was warned to be off the streets.'

'I've been to the library.'

'An educated Coloured, *geleerde Hotnot*. You've been to the bar. Look how drunk you are.'

'I'm not drunk. I don't drink.'

'Shut-up. *Hou jou bek, Hotnot.*'

A kick landed. He was bounced from one policeman to the other. Satchel ripped out of his hands. Contents on the ground. Was he watching a replay of the Dr. Jay incident? Wat it really happening to him?

'Communist books, hey?'

The books and papers were trampled on. Eric watched his term's work disappear.

One policeman produced bottles of wine. He put one into Eric's satchel.

'You don't drink? What this wine doing in your bag?'

Eric opened his mouth to protest. The other policeman had

opened a bottle. He poured the wine into Eric's mouth and over his clothing.

'Don't be so greedy. You can't drink quick enough. Why do you spill so much? Look at your clothes.'

'Constable, do you think this man is drunk?'

'Stinking drunk!'

Eric looked like a confused little boy between the burly policemen. He was often mistaken for one of the senior students. His students called him 'the absent-minded professor' because he was always lost in his own world. He was more comfortable with books than people. At home he was adored by his two sisters who never failed to wait up for him every night. His parents still protected him as if he were in junior school.

'Come from the library? Where's your books? Only a bottle of wine. *Dronklap,* drunkard.'

'*Sies!* You're stinking. All Coloureds drink cheap wine.'

Handcuffs slapped on.

Eric tried to say something. The policemen were enjoying their jokes and did not want to be interrupted. One slapped him across the face. Knocked his glasses off.

'Come, *jong kom.* We're not going to carry you. You have to walk. Are you too drunk to walk? We'll drag you.'

Eric decided to comply. The humiliating parade up Main Road and Church Street to the police station must be endured.

Into the fleapit.

'You, punk, do you enjoy pissing over somebody? Being piss-drunk you have enough for your show. Sies. You're too weak to say no to that pig! Mr. Tough, like hell.'

Eric heard one of the women trying to put an end to the show.

'You enjoyed the show before.'

'Yes, you and another Mr. Tough. You both looked stupid.'

'I'll do it to you if you don't shut up. Then your Evening-in-pissland-Paris will smell real good.'

A flashing knife signalled a free-for-all. Some of the regulars took their chance to land a few blows on the policemen in the scramble. The policemen had to take the blows during their efforts to restore order.

Eric wished he had the courage to land a few on those policemen as he crawled to the side of the cell to avoid the feet and fists as best he could.

Creator

Julian deWette

The childless ache to bear
beyond the edge of town
where the lathe-master turns smooth spindles, candlesticks
and two-toned spinning tops; yellow wood
sandwiched between ebony
without a trace of seam.
Growing forms hug the shaving blade;
the hand leans gently
to shape tiny skull indentations,
elastic sternum measured for breath after breath.
Then the putting-on of flesh; rounded mouth for crying,
fingers, too perfect yet for grasping;
dimpled foot arches fan out into toes so tiny
they had to have been imagined.

Christmas 1976

Barbara Masekela

In the Golden City
Sacrifice is once more
At firing hand
Young blood spurts on
Fanatic celebrants
Dressed in camouflage
Extend the rituals
These ceremonies of death
May rage on to another Dingane's day
These rivers of blood
Could flood over the high walls
Not too soon
Into the manicured gardens

Here in New York
Recorded voices croon
A white Christmas
Puppets at Schwartz grow
More human than the Fifth Avenue mobs
That doll in the window
Tagged five-hundred dollars
Smiles mocks
My seven hundred children dead

Snow
White silence
The quiet rain of foreign parts
Cannot powder sunshine memories
Shall not wind a shroud
Round my South Africa yearnings

Uthekwane

Barbara Masekela

I still fetch the pain
Waft in and out of it
Exorcizing demon memories
And a bloody fetus of love
Shot with pain
I accept

I miss it too
Your smile that spread
Cloaked my reason
Your absence is a thorn
Quick and sharp
On my left heart
In between my breasts
Where your head
Used to nestle

Demon Exile

Barbara Masekela

My resolve is outstared
Mother-hunger
Father-craving
Sister hankering
Myriad blood longings
Mushroom
Mount me here
On needle point
Labeled self reliance

My scarred face alien mask
Shaded and rouged
Jumps at me
In crowded windows
Concealed mirrors
Reflect eyes raised in inquiry
At an impostor rushing towards me
Blurred in a tremble
And unshed tears
We merge in the sound
Of splintering glass

Where are they now

Barbara Masekela

Where are they now
My people surrounded by the waters
At The-Cape-of-no-Good-Hope
The lifers at Robben Island
Whose words banned by order
Travel in sudden choirs
Of adolescent voices
Raising apartheid death a dare
Where the silenced ones
At the back of whose eyes
Years leap up
Stand at attention
Abandoning them
In the rigid minutes of waiting

| What Words |

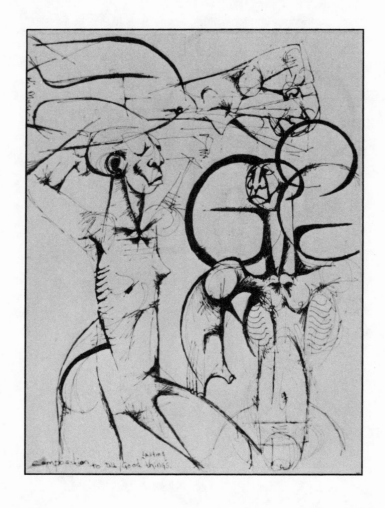

Foreign Body

Arthur Nortje
from *Lonely Against the Light*

Through the hole of the eye your virgin
germ has entered my sensitive skull.
Who told me to be curious, skirting
strange and ominously still waters?

Someone who looks and goes away is lucky.
In the jade enigma I tossed a pebble:
ripples breasted my feet, ran round and on.
Disturbance yielded nothing from the deep levels.

The only thing to stir it with one's hands.
Dusk came smokily to mingle
gentle obscurities. I rubbed my eye,
thinking it better to be a frog or otter.

The germ lodges like a young grain
in the gloomy oyster of the soul.
What substance round the foreign body
can pearl it smooth, what words can make me whole?

Oxford, January 1966

To Whom It May Concern

Sidney Sepamla
from *Hurry Up To It!*

Bearer
Bare of everything but particulars
Is a Bantu
The language of a people in southern Africa
He seeks to proceed from here to there
Please pass him on
Subject to these particulars
He lives
Subject to provisions
Of the Urban Natives Act of 1925
Amended often
To update it to his sophistication
Subject to the provisions of the said Act
He may roam freely within a prescribed area
Free only from the anxiety of conscription
In terms of the Abolition of Passes Act
A latter-day amendment
In keeping with moon-age naming
Bearer's designation is Reference number 417181
And (he) acquires a niche in the said area
As a temporary sojourner
To which he must betake himself
At all times
When his services are dispensed with for the day
As a permanent measure of law and order
Please note
The remains of R/N 417181
Will be laid to rest in peace
On a plot
Set aside for Methodist Xhosas
A measure also adopted
At the express request of the Bantu
In anticipation of any faction fight
Before the Day of Judgment.

A Poem

Mongane Serote
from *Tsetlo*

Everyone of us
throbs footsteps inside the chest of the earth
for we belong there

The earth is always tight-lipped
but only talks to itself
perturbed by its throbs.

Each of us will answer
when the worms dig in and out us for the truth,
below the earth.

Sharpeville

Dennis Brutus
from *Strains*

What is important
about Sharpeville
is not that seventy died:
nor even that they were shot in the back
retreating, unarmed, defenseless

and certainly not
the heavy calibre slug
that tore through a mother's back
and ripped into the child in her arms
killing it

Remember Sharpeville
bullet-in-the-back day

Because it epitomized oppression
and the nature of society
more clearly than anything else;
it was the classic event

Nowhere is racial dominance
more clearly defined
nowhere the will to oppress
more clearly demonstrated

what the world whispers
apartheid declares with snarling guns
the blood the rich lust after
South Africa spills in the dust

Remember Sharpeville
Remember bullet-in-the-back day

And remember the unquenchable will for freedom
Remember the dead
and be glad

At A Funeral

Dennis Brutus
from *A Simple Lust*

Black, green and gold at sunset: pageantry
And stubbled graves: expectant, of eternity,
In bride's-white, nun's-white veils the nurses gush
      their bounty
Of red-wine cloaks, frothing the bulged dirging
      slopes
Salute! Then ponder all this hollow panoply
For one whose gifts the mud devours, with our
      hopes.

Of all you frustrate ones, powers tombed in dirt,
Aborted, not by Death but carrion books of birth
Arise! The brassy shout of Freedom stirs our earth;
Not Death but death's-head tyranny scythes our
      ground
And plots our narrow cells of pain defeat and
      dearth:
Better that we should die, than that we should lie
      down.

    (Valencia Majombozi, who died shortly
      after qualifying as a doctor)

Another Alexandra

Mongane Serote
from *Tsetlo*

the skies and god's mystery look on
the blood flows
the tears dry
the screams are mute
and the mothers now depart
their doeks falling awkwardly over their faces
and their heads are bowed
the slaughter sheep hangs from a tree like the setting sun
here,
it is only children who still laugh and play and jump
as they play on the rabble heap;
Alexandra,
the streets are now closed
the doors
windows
poked out while the little girl stands there licking her lips
scratching her grey thigh
dazed by her child and adult experiences locked so tight in her
                                                            little head
where her innocence has been snatched;
Alexandra,
this little girl clutched a crying child in her arms and heard its
                                                    heart beat on her back
and tricked into sleep
while she was playing with rag-dolls
and longed to be held by the hand and told stories,
and the men sit on the stoep staring straight into space
wearing blank expressions
not even noticing women passing
Alexandra,
it is true that women have come to know
they know that graves are not only below the earth
where worms are so well informed, wearing mocking smiles
                                        everytime they hear us sing hymns

these women—
they sweat
their sweat drips in thick dart-drops big as their staring eyes
where sweet smiles still appear;

Alexandra,
if love is pain
this i have carried inside my loins
as i walked
fell
intoxicated
and fucked-up right inside the pitch of all that's me
watching
listening
even to concubines conspiring in secrets with husbands
and
i have heard a murder declared while we sat on a broken sofa
drinking
while i slept drunk, my heart shook like a tornado-uprooted
                                                              tree
as the whores scream whirled in the dark
and i heard a man weep like a woman giving birth
while he pleaded for his life;

Alexandra,
i have seen what i have seen
for
me, i was born with open eyes
to bleed my heart like a licking tin
and the blood is messy on my lap where i wring my hands
                                                 absent mindedly
while your streets fade
and your houses tumble like that
your face is twisted like a woman's riddled with bloody pain
for now,
the graves gape—

Alexandra,
i give you my back now, the secrets are in my heart and on
my lap
i cannot look
for your legs are chained apart
and your dirty petticoat is soaked in blood
blood from your ravaged wound.

ERA

Jaki Seroke
from *Staffrider*

some were engirthed with a canopy
of remorse some among us cried
like crocodiles some listened to the hokum
of 'instigators and tomato sauce' some
licked their fingers after a clutch

at the burnt bridges others immediately
dumped everything another slipped down
with the night other faces went
stony in twilight's eye yet
another preferred to baas this dragon's land.

I waited for you last night

Zindzi Mandela

from *Black As I Am*

I waited for you last night
I lay there in my bed
like a plucked rose
its falling petals my tears

the sound that my room
       inhaled
         drew in softly
         swallowed
in my ears
was the tapping on the window

getting up
I opened it
and a moth flew in
powdering my neck
shrugging
I caught its tiny wings
and kissed it
I climbed back into bed
with it
and left it to flutter around my head

I waited for you last night

Dimbaza

Austin Cloete
from *Black Voices, Shout*

Empty graves lie open to the sun
awaiting a starved corpse
while mothers cry and beat their breasts
and feet are blistered by hot earth

The same earth is cracked
like raw, festering wounds
dried up and scorched
by a menacing sun
give nothing but thorn bushes
whose sharp spears
burst from ochred rocks

They cry for food—they pray and wait
as many mothers did with sob-filled eyes
wait for tomorrow
when another child
claims an open grave
marked by a "white" cross

The Echoes
Of Breaking

James Matthews

the echoes of breaking
bones
are the bell-tones i hear
screams of pain shred my
ears
washed in their blood i
am
living is not a lie
my cell a gathering of
souls
consigned to a hell shared
pain, flowers draped upon
flesh
living is not a lie
bathed in my sister's
smile
i smelled my brother's
breath
i touched his flesh
death for me is not a
threat
living is not a lie

Requiem For My Mother

Keorapetse Kgositsile
from *Places And Bloodstains*

As for me
The roads to you
Lead from any place
Woman dancer-of-steel
Mother daughter sister
Of my young years
The roads to you
Lead from any place
I am.
        I do not know
If you hollered in delirium
Like an incontinent dotard
I do not know if you gasped
For the next breath, gagging
Fighting to hold your life in
I do not know if you took
Your last breath with slow resignation
But this I know

I dare not look myself
In the eye peeled red
With despair and impotent regret
I dare not look myself
In the ear groaning
Under these years and tears
I dare not mourn your death
Until I can say without
The art of eloquence
Today we move we move

As for me I will
Never again see the slow
Sadness of your eye
Though it remains
Fixed and talks

Through a grave I do not know
I teeter through
The streets of our anguish
Through this incontinent time and referent
And when I try to Scream *Vengeance*
My voice limps under the cacophony
Of them whose tongue is glued
To the bloodstains in the imperial
Monster's hallways and appetite

As for me
The roads to you
Lead from any place
Though I will never again
Know the morning odor
Of your anxious breath!
Don't let the sun shine
In your arse my child
We do not do those things
Though I will never again
Know your armpit odor
Before the ready-for-work mask
Though I will never again
See the slow sadness of your smile
Under the sun
Woman mother daughter sister
The slow sadness in your eye
Remains fixed and talks
Even here where the amber bandages
Of the sun kiss the day
Before they disappear beyond
These whitehooded mountains and appetites

Untitled

Barbara Masekela

You glowed in dim places
Whispering shimmering poetry
Inbetween studied anecdotes
Punctuated by too-prompt laughter
Now and then
False notes blared
I pressed down doubt
Stretched rules
Smoothed out wrinkles
In the idyll play

Now I sit here
Crouched over my memories
Hugging them close
In trembling thighs
Begging for forgetfulness
And the wings of a bird

| New Age |

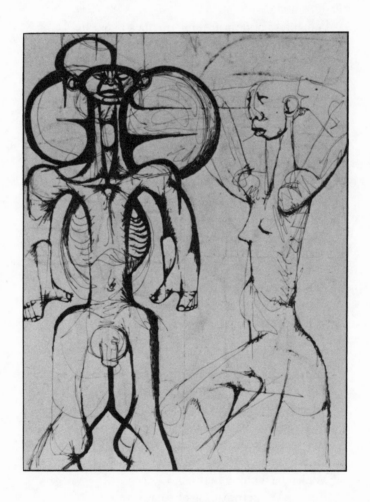

New Age

Keorapetse Kgositsile

The questions which have always been here
Jump at us like impatient lovers
Of nights which cannot be numbed
Not even by spirits departed by bottle or land

When fogs of despair jump up thick in our heads
When struggle becomes the next bottle
Or the warmth between a willing woman's thighs
Sucking into her our hasty greed
Remember O comrade commander of the ready smile
This is pain and decay of purpose

Remember in baton boot and bullet ritual
The bloodhounds of Monster Vorster wrote
SOWETO over the belly of my land
With the indelible blood of infants
So the young are no longer young
Not that they demand a hasty death

The past is also turbulent
Ask any traveller with memory
To tame it today is our mission
With liberty hammered to steel in our eye

Remember O Poet
When some of your colleagues meet
They do not talk the glories of the past
Or turn their tongues backwards
In platitudes or idealistic delirium
About change through chance or beauty
Or the perversion you call love
Which be nothing nothing
But the Western pairing of parasites

The young whose eyes carry neither youth nor cowardice
The workers whose song of peace

Now digs graves for the goldfanged fascists monsters
With artistic precision and purpose
Now know the past is turbulent
We must tame it now
Ask any eye fuelled with liberty

Tell those with ears to hear tell them
Tell them my people are a garden
Rising out of the rancid rituals of rape and ruin
Tell them tell them in the dry season
Leaves will dry and fall to fertilize the land
Whose new flowers black green and gold
Are a worker's song of fidelity
To the land that mothered you

Austin Moving-Along Ballad

Dikeni Bayi
from *GAR*

Under the Austin stars down by the Armadillo
they shared a frosted pitcher and fierce jalapenos
    while their bodies blazed—
there was sweet smoke and country music in the air

but somewhere there was a war
and he heard guns in his head,
there were children crying
and friends were dying
so he sang, sadly, a moving-along song.

On a summer night under a buttermilk sky
near I-H 35 where police patrolled suspiciously
they lay in the warm grass while stars danced
       like fireflies

but somewhere there was a war
and he heard guns in his head,
there were children crying
and friends were dying
so he sang, sadly, a moving-along song.

Sunday morning down in Flapjack Canyon
in line for hot cakes and slow trickling syrup
there was sweetness in the air,
    on their hands and their mouths

but somewhere there was a war
and he heard guns in his head,
there were children crying
and friends were dying
so he sang, sadly, a moving-along song.

Under the stars in the Theater-in-the-Park
sprawled on the turf in casual abandon
they laughed at Juliet's horniness while their
       bodies twined

but somewhere there was a war
and he heard guns in his head,
there were children crying
and friends were dying
so he sang, sadly, a moving-along song.

In the chill night by the sleaze of the sad East-side
they clasped in an embrace that stilled the world forever
but a train hooted from the desolate tracks

and somewhere there was war
and he heard guns in his head,
there were children crying
and friends were dying
so he moved along singing a moving-along song.

Phantoms

Barbara Masekela

Your touch remembered
Bursts through
Swells
Opening my eyes still
Dawns of forty pillow rains
Murmur your voice
Thrust me into ancient deserts
Hiccup wastelands silent
Where sands undulate
Gritty breezes whisper
Forevermore "no more"
and
Unyielding sun
Proffers a mirage of you
                    only

All Hungers Pass Away

Somehow we survive

Dennis Brutus
from *A Simple Lust*

Somehow we survive
and tenderness, frustrated, does not wither.

Investigating searchlights rake
our naked unprotected contours;

over our heads the monolithic decalogue
of fascist prohibition glowers
and teeters for a catastrophic fall;

boots club the peeling door.

But somehow we survive
severance, deprivation, loss

Patrols uncoil along the asphalt dark
hissing their menace to our lives,

most cruel, all our land is scarred with terror,
rendered unlovely and unlovable;
sundered are we and all our passionate surrender

but somehow tenderness survives.

A Piano Toccata
by Baldassare Galuppi

Dennis Brutus

from *Salutes & Censures*

Such a melancholy
rises
like the wry scent of wilted roses
or titian-haired beauties
their heads drooping:
tears, or despair, or decay

O those creamy carrara breasts,
mouths bruised with much loving
falling cadences, tired hearts, dying strains

March 5, 1980
After the music and a Browning poem. d.b.

It Is Night

James Matthews

It is night
it has long been night
in the hearts of mothers
who have seen their fruit
thrust back into the soil

It is night
and the darkness covers
the shame in the eyes
of fathers with crushed spirits
who stand like clipped trees
stripped of proud foliage

It is night and children stir restlessly
under night's ebony cover
the torment that grips them
shapes their limbs into
patterns of foreboding

Night will pass
and mothers accept their pain
as the shame of fathers
will be hidden from sight
but the children will greet dawn
with a fire of their own

All Hungers Pass Away . . .

Arthur Nortje

from *Lonely Against the Light*

All hungers pass away,
we lose track of their dates,
desires arise like births,
reign for a time like potentates.

I lie and listen to the rain
hours before full dawn brings
forward a further day and winter sun
here in a land where rhythm fails.

Wanly I shake off sleep,
stare in the mirror with dream-puffed eyes,
drag my shrunken corpulence
among the tables of rich libraries.

Fat hardened in the mouth,
famous viands tasted like ash:
the mornings after of a sweet escape
ended over bangers and mash.

I gave those pleasures up,
the sherry circuit, arms of some bland girl.
Drakensberg lies swathed in gloom.
Starvation stalks the farms of the Transvaal.

What consolation comes
drips away as bitterness.
Blithe footfalls pass my door
as I recover from the wasted years.

The rain abates. Face-down
I lie, thin arms folded, half-aware
of skin that tightens over pelvis.
Pathetic, this, the dark posture.

December 1970

Seaparankoe

Keorapetse Kgositsile

The need of the land we sing, the flowers
Of manhood, of labor, of spring;
We sing the deaths that we welcome as ours
And the birth from the dust that is green we sing.
                                        —*Cosmo Pieterse*—

Malome your body has followed Duma's
In less than the nine months
That follow the blood of the moon
Bidding the mother to usher humanity here

Your body is down under now
Down under Seaparankoe
And predictably there are fools here
Who still cannot know that
The Kotanekind can neither fall nor fail

Our hearts and heads
Remain pliable in the easy embrace
Of your worldwide hands
For generations they will remain
Pliable like dough
Turning to bread
In the worker's hands
Or words turning
To embers of wisdom and courage
At the bidding of the poet's heart

But Seaparankoe the mouths of fools
Who do not know that
No power on this planet
Could ever kill humanity
Or stay our desire for liberty and peace
Are here with us
From the perverse core of their greed

Every person must work or fight
That is the simple truth we learn
From your life and love
Which rules and enhances our vision
Out of the lethal stench of the intemperate present

Here I do not bury or freeze my tears
Salty as the sea accomplice
In the crime and rancid slime
Of pogroms class clashes genocide
Across the taut belly of this planet

Under your vision which commands
Our conscience and consciousness
With easy affection as my brother tells
I say yes to the tears and the sea
I say yes and fashion them
Into the instrument and fruit
Of our informed and determined
Want and purpose
I say yes Malome
We must be bolshevised
I say yes
Every person must work or fight
I say yes
Kotane is dead
But Kotanekind can neither fall nor fail

Come Malome Come
Come we say not that we are dotard
Enough to think we can bring back the dead
Kotanekind come bind us
Come bind the poets
Come make of our music
The sound of the gun
That will set us free

To create to laugh to work
And sing the deaths that we welcome as ours
And the birth from the dust that is green
Not that we are strangers to fear
But we love freedom and peace more
And for this we work and fight

Straight Ahead

For My Unborn Child

Baleka Kgositsile

Mound of life
　　　rise like tide of revolution
Mound of life
　　　come join us
　　　as sure as the day of liberation

Lands far from your forefathers'
embrace you and feed you
as they will
it is not your fault
but it will be a crime
if in your lifetime
you do not fight
back to the land of your forefathers

My screams go up
　　　the labour of my people
The pain
　　　the struggle
　　　the blood
The cry of determination
　　　from the bottom of the pile
　　　the women of our land
Life on the beautiful land

'There is no birth without blood'
There is no blood without pain
　　　　　I add
When the streets and rivers of our land turn red
　　　it will be the dawn of the day
　　　our land will kiss freedom welcome

I labour with all the mothers
　　　whose children's cherished lives
Were ended with a callous ease
　　　known only by a fascist

To them I bear hundreds of sons
    who will be Africa's sun
To the fascist I scream
    the labour of my people
The pain
    the struggle
    the blood
The scream of my people's determination
    splits fascist eardrums

Exhausted by the battle of labour
    with untold satisfaction
    I kiss you welcome
With dreams and hopes
    born with each determined kick and move
    with each ripple of my stomach
    like the anger of my people
Mound of life
    come join us
Together we must hunt the fascist down
    cut his deaf head off
    and let life flow in our land

Isandhlwana Incarnate

Bheki Langa

hearts torn from souls
bleeding warm
blood sinking with soul
into greedy soil
bodies ripped into shreds
twitching from
nuclear death cells
then the final convulsive retch
the brain still recording . . .

police vans
swallow the wounded
death overflows trenches
handcuffs sink into proud flesh
and the journey to the death cells
begins amid shouts of
amandla!
fists resolute
in spite of handcuffs

demonstrations violently crushed
but our songs can never be hushed
for the exclamation marks
of our slogans
land resoundingly on boer pigheads
like knobkieries
the struggle is food
age-old rule of bloodhounds
gives birth to revolt
the sharp teeth of class struggle
chew off whole epochs

we have travelled a long way
in soweto
we were matadors

tricking bullnosed war tanks
and learned
how much a brick
can bleed a bullet to death
the vaudeville flatfooted
enthusiasm of hired killers
vanished in a stonemaze
and groans crept
through stoneheaps

on bare incarnate rims
we chestheave on
under napalm glare
of sunbaked roads
wringing our intestines dry
whilst steel bats
spit death from treetops
caught in blizzards
of lizards creeping
military green wizards
a shower of hope
from the AK for the MK
when we take aim
we salute not dead stone
but living spirit and blood
sandhlwana incarnate

In the Black Gut

Mongane Serote

I want to talk to black people
Talk like a block of ice melting on their bellies,
The water cold like a corpse,
Dam round their navels,
Kill the warmth they sucked in their mother's stomachs,
Kill the kindness
Kill the shit about being human,
Kill the fear
Wake them up to what they are,
Smiling -
Smiles. smiles
Smiling to the death of their kind,
Smiling,
Intoxicated by fumes in a shebeen
Talking shit,
Intoxicated by blood of brother dying in the streets:
And babies born of rape
born of drunken stupor
Honour! I said honour!
Honour to those polygamous bastards, who died with time,
Honour to those bloody men who were schooled on the mountain.
Love to you black women of old,
You who closed eyes and blew into the smoke and flames came
      leaping,
You who threw the child on your back,
And brushed your bare-feet against the hot sands,
Love to you,
Tears to you and my old woman,
For having a son like my father.

In Memoriam

Pascal Gwala

How much does one do
to be with his people?
In heart and soul?
Nthuli, you clenched
your black fist,
and did it amongst the people.
They were with you.
They still are.
You did not confound them
with ready known truths
- unlike those
only yesterday non-white;
today, from behind
catchphrases and cliches;
now clad in Afro style
aloof from the people,
want to teach them
how to be Black
to those, though years
of agonies and betrayals,
have been as Black
as the oracle
that has always said:
One day Blacks shall be free;
free and liberated.
No, you are with the people
They live with you.
Live Black Hero;
In our minds and deeds
We watch you say,
Live Black man, Live!

Poem

Christine Douts

Our mothers are weeping
the wailing is spiralling
dissolving into the sky
roofing the open graves
of their sons and daughters
knifed
    slashed
        raped
Our mothers are crying
moist rivulets of despair
are running down the folds
of their dark skins
their sons and daughters
are
    imprisoned
        beaten
            hanged
for sins not theirs

Our mothers
with their empty eyes
and busy hands
are the unheralded heroines
of our nation
the unsung martyrs of our struggle
their tears shall flow into a river
the river shall
fold over every curve of our land
drowning the sinner in his sins
saturating us with pride
our mothers shall sing lullabies
in the golden fields of the land
Africa shall be ours
Our mothers shall be what they are

Only To You

Ilva Mackay

Phase I

Your love is the rain,
it patters on the roof of my soul
it ravages and rapes my fields
it erodes deep dongas in my lands
and gets lost in the eternity of words.

Your love is the sun,
it glitters on my earth-coloured face
it ripens the seed which is ready to burst
it enhances my bubbling, bursting, beautiful black being
then radiates our happiness into the dingy alley where we live.

Phase II

WITH
YOU who travel in the top deck of buses
        who live in a box, or is it a house?
        who receives a coloured education
I
        who am degraded from day to day
        who am allowed merely to exist
        who eat Friday's bread on Monday
WANT TO SHARE TOMORROW.

Phase III

Your mind is deep
                deep
                        deep
dark as the dungeons
dark.
Its unknown depths are painted black
                        black
            as the white man's sins black.

I want to be with you
who live in sandy streets
of dirt and death.

I long for you
who laugh amidst murderous manslaughter
yet still continue to laugh

I need you
who sleep alongside
drunkenness and despondency.

UNFOLD
your mind
your dark as the dungeons
      dark mind
your black as the white man's sins
      black mind.
Let me too share your life,
let me too sleep alongside you
who choose to lock me out.

A Prayer
For Africa

Song (We Sing)

Cosmo Pieterse
from *South African Voices*

We sing our sons who have died red
Crossing the sky where barbed wire passes
Bullets of white paper, nails of grey lead
And we sing the moon in its dying phases.

We sing the moon, nine blue moons of being
We sing the moons of barren blood
Blood of our daughters, waters fleeing
From bodiless eyes, that have stared and dried.

The seed of the land we sing, the flowers
Of manhood, of labor, of spring;
We sing the deaths we welcome as ours
And the birth from the dust that is green we sing.

A Journey

Mongane Serote
from *Tsetlo*

My feet feel weary
like a feather
Yet
I walk
this path that breaks the heels
I come on
my wet pores weeping
I—
I have peeled my muscles
looking for bread and water and a place to rest
I plod the paths
with my feet and arms and eyes
and all my body brandish pain
my heart took a flight out of me
it fell on the earth
Frantic
Searching
I—
I have went inside me
made love with the gaping wounds
and lost gut
lost in the terrible battle with fear

The Sounds Begin Again

Dennis Brutus

from *A Simple Lust*

The sounds begin again;
the siren in the night
the thunder at the door
the shriek of nerves in pain.

Then the keening crescendo
of faces split by pain
the wordless, endless wail
only the unfree know.

Importunate as rain
the wraiths exhale their woe
over sirens, knuckles, boots;
my sounds begin again.

A Prayer For Africa From the Mouths of Babies

Mandlenkosi Langa
from *MEDU*

look brothers of the hour
all these sewers
screaming and gurgling
our guilt
aborted babies
screaming babies their heads
gnawed by rats fattened in the dark corners
of our hearts

there is everywhere
this eye
baleful and unclosed seeing all
staring and staring
at all these shapes of all these
deaths
graves of the young ones
moulded with the clay
that makes up our bodies
burnt in kilns built
in the hours of africa's ignorance

Why is it that everywhere we go
we see ashes and ruins
why is everything so white
and so desolate
you see national skeletons
birthed by barrenness of leaders
on podiums
finishing their speeches with aplomb

the deafening applause
cannot be louder than the songs
sung on gravesites
but can be more silent
than the invocation of ashes to ashes

there is everywhere absence of calm
let there be no calm
let there be fire and brimstone
a *luta continua* doesn't mean
a looter continues
let there be africa walking upright!

Oxford
Journal

Oxford Journal

David Bunn, Chicago

These six poems are representative of the many finely-wrought draft versions to be found in Nortje's *Oxford Journals*. In the face of growing critical acclaim for Arthur Nortje's work the time is ripe for some of these unpublished pieces to meet an audience. The early enthusiasm for Nortje is now giving way to a more mature evaluation of one of South Africa's most urgent and brilliant voices; we look forward to the publication of a more complete version of his works.

Five of the poems are drawn from Nortje's earlier years— before he left for Oxford—and one from the later years abroad. *Exploration* is a brief but sharp portrayal of the "apartheid" generation and South Africa under Verwoerd. In the characteristic use of the image of the cycle of the seasons, the political environment is internalized as the "winter" of the heart. *Late Spring* and *Poem in Absence* make similar use of closely observed details and the lyric voice. The mind of the poet returns, time after time, to the figure of a woman who has the power to heal and transform the loneliness of the changing seasons.

Brief Thunder at Sharpeville and *Reflections* mark another recurrent theme in Nortje's verse: the death of statesmen, political violence, and harsh injustice are all set at some distance, in a strongly visualized context. Those who suffer often seem reduced to a lower but resilient form of life, waiting for the political climate to change. Of all the poems published here, *Courtnay Rocks* is perhaps the most interesting. This verse marks the end of the *Oxford Journals* and the tremendous burst of creative energy that spanned Nortje's four difficult years in England and Canada.

Exploration

in the barren mornings of winter i try
to shake out the cobwebs of nightmares,
to belch that room's miasma. i
try to laugh & my lips feel dry
above the heart that thumps regardless. Try

employment agencies, departments, bureaus;
standing long in the rag-&-bottle queue
on leaner lean days. Going back
it fails, my face is wrong. i try
to visit the lush park of the city council
with squirrels & fine young whites

under the Board of Executioners sign
a blond policeman with his leather holster
in the grounds of their houses of parliament

in the barren mornings of winter i try

K.1964

Brief Thunder at Sharpeville

Because one dead man does not make a summer
there are black hands in the sky that clamour,
faces that coolly stare from the concrete gloom.
Of my kind are many willing and able
to suffer the truncheon, to puzzle the jackboot.

Patrol this limbo day that swarms with people,
I being one of them. Meanwhile the sky,
grown grey with waiting, rumbles impatiently.
Clouds steel themselves for battle, which is common,
& clouds can never quarrel without weeping.

A squall of blobbing rain. Short argument,
stuttered out like gunfire;
So air is acrid with smoke & soil damp with blood.
Dead streets I notice, & not with terror:
I came out living. Of me there are many.

(4/64.)

Late Spring

Late spring scent, the taste still falls
short of perdurable flavour.
Sunlight diamonds the jade place
where snails keep their damp vigil.
In a green tunnel of ordeal
the warm day's edge is chill.

A fine blind fury of raindrops,
swansong lashed through the leaves, so
that winter now dies noble.
Muddled, the surf swells shoreward
with boom and crash that slowly
end in a beach curve, sand-kissed.

Though the heart's a continuum
& rhythms never in memory only
often the abrupt silences
of turtledoves filter from a vacuum.
Broken cadences in the air
remind of absences at empty moments.

Wake & wait: dew & opalescence
conceal the grass, the azure sky:
dreams perpetrate the promise
of summer that you made me crave
keenly, for all your reluctance .
I cherish these warm beginnings.

2/29/64

Reflections

Fogged morning, clockwork city
of sewers & towers, smoke & sirens.
Sad weather
engenders sombre reflections, reflects
in campanile bell that conveys the hours.

I am not infinite
shuffling my feet over cobbled
public squares where pigeons open
those flitting ranks that close behind me.

Skies change from opalescent
to their usual inscrutable blue,
then the shimmering turquoise water
lies under the hill of houses
despite the death of statesmen.
Or the lifting veil reveals
familiar buildings of glass & concrete,
no face or word or happy miracle.

Images shape but so often
wind stirs to ruffle the water;
grey ripples lip the sand, spume clings.
Gradually I let
slip my disappointment.
Wherever flotsam relaxes
black bacteria renew the action.

(Port Elizabeth. 1965.)

Poem in Absence

Final honeysuckles flame in hedges,
wafting orange, plumed; the bitter leaves
quiver at autumn's crisp, acknowledge
summer's removal, loss of ease.

Sunset softens cloud with rose
& dusk spreads smokily lonely:
in the ruined valleys rise
the earth miasma. Stonily

I hunch in the dark & chill
bearing desolation & hunger:
the pain has grown occasional.
Yet when the rare ache lingers
I strain towards that miracle
your exquisite healing fingers.

K. 1965

on the treetrunk looking towards the coastal
mountains across the noon tide you can see
sunlit snow, mauve haze, a pastel day
& try to capture the soul of august:

listenable music of the crabshell
in the caverns of the rocks with water trickle:
you may wonder what the crows
are doing at the water's edge
curious by the mudholes of crustaceans.
Evening boats are resting in the beach-house
above the empty channels.

In the indian village maybe
they are busy on the dollar trade of curios
for tourist shops, mythologies
of killer whale, of beaver, & of raven,
of eagle, bear, & salmon. This old totem

pole defies analysis, land creature
washed nightly by the waters, its white branches
buried in the shore grass & the seaweed
draped along its blunt roots. Frail
cobwebs stir at leeward in the noon breeze
suspended from dead knots & dead projections:
                                     the white and wasted
limb makes a magnificent
seat for serendipity.

Summer of 67

| Long Road |

No More Strangers

Mongane Serote
from *PECULEF Newsletter*

it is us, it is us
the children of soweto
langa, kagiso, alexandra, gugulethu and nyanga
us
a people with a long history of resistance
us
who dare the mighty
for it is freedom, only freedom which can quench our thirst—
we did learn from terror that it is us who will seize history
our freedom.

remember
as though motherless or even lifeless
how we walked the night
the loveless streets
owned by so cruel such merciless emissaries who speak foreign
            tongues
who turned us against each other
remember—
ask any child or mother
who are penned in the night of the system
ask any father
about the weight of despair
about the assault of fear on love
when gunfire shatters the night
and the running, terrified footsteps merge with the heartbeat
a heartbeat gone mad with terror
for so many nights
so many nights, so many of us have slipped with such swiftness
from life to death
for so many cruel deaths
on the mean streets of such merciless nights and days
remember
how you or i or any one of us
with a voluptuous lust for death

how we got drunk
with whiskey, dagga and religions
remember the shattering despair to feel as worthless as debris
remember the shades of death we longed for
here we are now

we think of nights behind us
when the children were shot, when their blood was spilled
when their little bodies rolled on the streets
rolled as if stones gone mad rolling from the mountains
remember how they charged, the children charged and fell
here we go again
a man or a woman
out of the insatiable stomachs of vampires called factories
walks the night soaked with the blood of children
walks weary on a friday night
to where?
do not tell us of soweto, alexandra, langa, nyangam athlone,
bonteheuwel or witbank
the ember of the blood of our children has turned these to ashes
it were us it is us
who were taught by history
that terror before the will of the people
is like a sheep in the mouth of a crocodile
here we go again
we have learnt from so many cruel nights
that oppressors are guilty forever
and we know that we will move.

it will be the trees, the mountains
it will be the silence of the karroo and its heat
it will be the song of our rivers
moving us one with them
moving
the night giving us sanctuaries
the day witness but silent

it will be us
steel-taut to fetch freedom
and—
we will tell freedom
we are no more strangers now.

Guerrilla

Cosmo Pieterse
from *South African Voices*

I sometimes feel a cold love burning
Along the shuddering length of all my spine;
It's when I think of you with some kind of yearning,
Mother, stepmotherland, who drop your litter with a bitter
    spurning.

And then I know, quite quietly and sure, just how
Before the land will take new seed, even before we forge a single
    plough,
We'll have to feel one sharp motion deep, resolve one deed:
That we must march over the length of all your life, transgressing
    your whole body with harsh boots upon our feet.

But even then there must also remain somewhere within your
    tissued depth
    Some little corners of an undisguised
        motherliness to bleed
Warmth in which we may dream sleep, where we might
    cling and find remission, help;
    on which our deeds may feed their hunger unsurprised,
        to which our suffering needs
    even and all our deaths must lead.

The Long Road: The Tunnel

Victor Matlou

there is light down there at the end of the tunnel
this here road man hang on its liver
smiling and insulting
cupping life in clenched palms
we move on relentlessly on this road
full of chains
heavy the step and the fall
but robust the fervent loins
that bear the way

there is light down there at the end of the tunnel
to grope on to touch to carve hopes
breathe songs into hearts of martyrs
to dry tears to summon the dead
to life
hoorah to the light down there
at the end of the tunnel
man must sing to drown the horror
of the pilgrimage step to success

the road mute and noisy
rising at every fall steadfast
completing circles that must begin
levelling landmarks that man has created
calling and culling maturity
pointing out there at the light
at the end of the tunnel

the tunnel rough and taunting
has many corners
ready to hide all the hides of cowardice
but there is a persistent voice here
long and short the measure of the tunnel
coaxing men and women of form
who care to begin
for it is this beginning that the road
is all about

at the end of the tunnel
light begins
and mothers to the fingers of light
shall not stop to cry
here the funeral begins
at the end of the tunnel
down there where the light stands
fixed tottering in the hearts of man

this light i know
i saw it yesterday
covered in the eyes of a devil frightened
this light that has tortured its way
to the birth of my life
this light that interogates martyrs
having only the power to hammer
to season the will
hoorah to the intrigue of the light
that i know
i live with it here propping my elbows
talking to my wobbling knees
this light this road
when will the chains fall
cries . . .
there have been carpets of prayers
wishing and wishing
but the stars of the hearts of men
that have pierced the night of this road
have covered its surface
with a tarmac of spears
and boiling courage
come . . . where are the poets
to sing the glory of pain
to drown their pens with the iron letters of broken knees
and pumping hearts and proud heads
where are they . . . aah! ! . . . where are they

they have all gone down under the road
for only this road matters
those who remain have neither courage
nor skill
curse them

all my people are on this road
for this road is the road of life
of accommodation
running with and towards the light of life

and women give birth here
a choice in anguish
binding a generation to this road
hoorah to the women
the birth and the death
this road claims all
this road is harder than the road
that hurled me here
this road kills everybody to life

and choice
no chance to move without seeing
before you the light calls
but the stride is yours
and the fall sits on your nerves
this insolent road of roads

it is dusty here
where men have kicked before
and breathed
you listen with your ears
you listen what else

this road is long my dear
and our hands these hands
that have chosen to hang on its liver
must not tire
so come let's have our fingers in directed unison

not faith
calculated hoped practice
of eye-winks breaths and movements
in this road where men
find themselves thick
in the belly of the beast

can you hear
the roar
the laughter
cracking bones can you hear

this is the seed of conquest
stripes of honour
this road
there is insult that sits on my skin
the leprosy that blurs my way
i must mature
lest i drag this road
skin deep

for this road can take many many forms
this road
this wild horse
bridle it and keep your eyes fixed
on the light at the end of the tunnel
there are temperate voices here
demanding
and the course where is the course

this road ages not
full of hard truth and the labour
full of echoes to be sifted
in these many many faces

this highway cruel road revolution
brooks no subways no by-paths
but what of these faces

these hearts
on the cuffs of my existence
what of them
the answer is the answer to the road
the light at the end of the tunnel

birds sing
and flowers bloom
and children break into smiles
and a heart cannot be stilled
you wait to take a breath
at the existing soft world
the love that you must fight for
of bright leaves
and loved ones
      and of HUMANITY
        take it ALL
for this is what the road is for

backed by labour
i have said what i wanted to say
in words
but the road is the finger
in the heart of man
and the light is always surrounded
by the dark

there are shadows here
that we must pick with the dust of time
to recreate a lost age to regain colour
call it anything if you may
but shadows haunt
like that light in the dark
disturbing
a disturbing road this is the road
the present the past
and the grand expectations

opening opening and opening
beyond the horizon there is light
a throne of the sun
but all that rests on man's ability
to can
to elbow life strings
to stand on tattered ruins
actualize hope to inhabit a citadel
even the ruins have shadows
and this road is no exception

come comrade
take this road this landscape
with the swoop of your heart
look
our people huddled together scattered
some waiting on death with smiles
their way is the way of the hare
hunted
but now no more
i shall go the way of the tiger
clawing the road biting and chewing
digesting salvation
this is the only way
for this distance is tough and cheeky
i'll not respect an inch
      until i chew it all
      until i chew it all

i am proud that i concluded
for conclusions
if they are conclusions and beginnings
mother action
this road is the road of action
all the tales told here
are tales against myths

real people reliving real people
in this real age of this season

my past is on the pulse of this road
but now the light burns clearer
i'll say no more of this
no more

this valley that i call my valley
my country sub divided cracked
i call upon hands the making fingers
to draw the sharpness
to put a spoor
there is no time here nor hill
that must stand on the way
for there is no way
except the way of the tiger
the committing road
the burning winners cross
the crossed fingers of the fisted road

on the shores of the river this river
there many a flowery site stand to dissuade
but the man of destiny decides
the measure of his hook
even here facing the light
man stands doomed to the anguish
of self-definition
and his road has meaning
when my toes hug the distance
my toes are history
seasons come and go
meeting every time
at the same time
where
at the point of my anguished toes

it is nice to talk like this
for man is afraid to look at the mute stones
and i say i exist
no . . . no . . .
let's have poets sort out embarrassments
to plot the portrait of nerves
and to say we are sane we are sane
even if the shores claim our psyche
the drunkenness to decide not to be
but this
in the thick of the road
the shore is full thick with the smell of fish
sitted on borrowed chairs
and the bells on their necks
direct maggots of time
            these casualties
            shall we stand and stare

and women give birth here
a choice in anguish
binding a generation to this road
my past is on the pulse of this road
there is light down there at the end of the tunnel
to grope on to touch to carve hopes
breathe songs into hearts of martyrs
to dry tears to summon the dead
to life

June 16 Year Of The Spear

Keorapetse Kgositsile

They call me freedomchild
I am liberationbound
My name is June 16
But this is not 1976

Freedomchild homewardbound
With an AK47 resting easy in my arms
The rivers I cross are no longer treacherous boundaries
Throwing me into the frustrating arms of exile
The rivers I cross are love strings
Around my homeland and me
Around the son and the new day

Who does not see me
Will hear freedomsound
Roaming the rhythms of my dream
Roosting warmly palpable as breast of every mother
Splitting every day and night
Spreading freedomseed all over this land of mine

My mothers fathers of my father kinsmen
Because I am June 16
And this is not Soweto 1976
I emerge in the asphalt streets of our want
And because 'my memory is surrounded by blood'
My blood has been hammered to liberationsong
And like Rebelo's bullets
And Neto's sacred hope
I am flowering
Over the graves of these goldfanged fascist ghouls
All over this land of mine

I am June 16
As Arab Ahmed says
My body is the fortress
Let the siege come!

I am the fireline
And I will besiege them
For my breast is the shelter
Of my people

I am June 16
I am Solomon Mahlangu
I am the new chapter
I am the way forward from Soweto 1976
I am poetry flowering with an AK47
All over this land of mine

Hanged

Dennis Brutus
from *Salutes& Censures*

*In Memoriam: Solomon Mahlangu Hanged
by the Apartheid Government, Pretoria
Dawn, April 6, 1979*

I
Singing
he went to war
and singing
he went to his death

II
There was sunlit
Goch Street
and the clear
pale blue sunlight
of the Highveld

and the sunlit bustle
of Edgar's Store
and the goodly things
money might buy
for the rich and white

and the overalled workers
delivery "boys"
messenger "boys"
sitting on curbs
with nowhere to rest

and the sharp crack
of gunfire
and screams of pain
and barked commands
the thud of falling bodies

Afterwards
there was the long grey corridor

the rattling salute on metal bars
the stark shape of the gallows
the defiant shouts of "Amandla"

Singing he went to war
and singing he went to his death

III
One simply poses
one's life
against another's
one's death
against another's death:

but the sides are different:
ours is life
joyous life
a free life, for the free
and theirs
is the monstrous life of a monstrous thing
who lives on the death of others
on our deaths

IV
The body buried secretly
in Mamelodi
and friends excluded
thousands of mourners barred

At the cemetery,
in Mamelodi
Mahlangu's mother
and thousands of friends
wait

The thousands waiting
weeping, angry
are told to disperse

The police announce
"The corpse you are waiting for
will not be delivered."

In the centre of Mamelodi
the police
swinging heavy rubber clubs
disperse 200 students
gathered to protest

Mahlangu knew
he might have to die:
he gave his life
for liberty.

V
(Eschel Rhoodie's father
was a hangman

the South African Secret Police
prowl the U.S. Campuses

their agents
function as academics

they hire mercenaries
as their hitmen

—Mr. and Mrs. Smit lie bullet-riddled
beside their family hearth—

their ruthless desperation
has no limit on criminality

theirs
and their corporate bosses)

VI
In the dimly-lit
mostly empty auditorium

the curious nervous
attentive crowd

the careful welcomes
focus mainly on me

there are complaints
of college harassment

the Dean of Spies
is falsely cordial

I pour scorn on stooge Mobutu
challenge Uncle Tom Sullivan

I evoke Mandela, Biko
Sharpeville and Soweto

a shooting in Johannesburg
stone-breaking on Robben Island

Solomon
Mahlangu

His gallant life
His gallant death

VII
Blue spruce
White pine
Yellow poplars

a weak dawn
seeps red
over the Appalachian foothills

here
blacks and slaves were brought
as strikebreakers

now
the subdued miners
can oppress minorities

ahead
red-raw lumber
scattered on the road

and overturned trailer
wheels in the air
like a docile beagle's paws

a driver
his head severed;
a death in the dawn

VIII
On the road
to the airport
I search the news
till I find the dread item;
He was hanged at dawn

IX
All night
his name
his face
his body
his fate
the cell
the gallows
pressed on my awareness
like a nail
hammered in my brain

Solomon
Mahlangu

till dawn
till the time
till the news
the newspaper report

he had been hanged

then the nail
was pulled from my brain
and the drip
of tears inside my skull
began

X
Singing
he went
to war
and singing
he went
to his death

A Luta Continua
(Requiem for Duma Nokwe)

Keorapetse Kgositsile

Duma, child of my mother,
Your body has left us, yes
That is a boundary
We had not expected so soon
You taught us, though, that boundaries
And oceans merely separate people bodily

There are men, Che said,
Who find their hereafter
Among the people
Life and victory as you knew
And lived it in all the "names
That in dying for life
Make life surer than death"
Will continue to spring and flower
From mother's womb and earth's bowels
From hand of warrior and worker too

If the warped bloodhounds of tyranny say
They will torture and kill us
Let them. Let them
Skulls they will crack, yes
Young bones they will trample underfoot, yes
School and church will also try
To twist and break our young yearning minds, yes
But the unbridled brutality of these beasts
Shall not break us. We are not twigs
Your love for humanity and peace
Strengthens us. We now clearly know
'A Worker's world is ascending'

Duma, child of my mother,
There are men who find their hereafter
Among the people
You live forever in us
You are the names

That in dying for life
Make life surer than death

Poet, leave him alone you have praised him
If you sing of workers you have praised him
If you sing of liberation you have praised him
If you sing of brotherhood you have praised him
If you sing of peace you have praised him
You have praised him without knowing his name
His name is Spear of the Nation. MAYIBUYE!

Appendix

The Banning of Staffrider
Vol. 2 No. 1—March 1979: Two Letters

The following represents the rationale behind the wretched Apartheid system's censoring of creative expression and its resultant reply by the editors of Staffrider magazine.

A LETTER TO THE PUBLISHERS FROM THE PUBLICATIONS DIRECTORATE

Dear Sirs,

PUBLICATIONS ACT, 1974: PUBLICATION: 'STAFFRIDER'—VOL. 2, NO. 1, MARCH 1979

In reply to your letter dated 4 April 1979, I have to inform you that the committee's reasons for declaring that the above-mentioned publication is undesirable within the meaning of section 47 (2) (e) of the Publications Act, 1974, were as follows:

1. *Introductory remarks*: The publication is a literary magazine providing writers and poets (mostly Black) with a medium of expression. It is published by Ravan Press, Braamfontein, and printed by Zenith Press of the same address. The quality of the paper and the printing is high, and the publication is probably heavily subsidized. These factors, of course, do not in themselves add up to undesirability. This is the fifth consecutive issue to come before the committee. The first one was found to be undesirable under *setion 47 (2) (a), (d) and (e)*. Several of the subsequent issues were found to contain material of a doubtful nature, but the committee decided that, on balance, they could be let through. The present issue, however, does not fall into this category, and the committee has found it to be undesirable under *section 47 (2) (e)*. This does not, however, imply that every article, poem or illustration is necessarily undesirable, and does not prohibit them being published separately or in another publication.

2. In assessing the present publication the committee took into consideration favourable factors such as—that protest literature is an acknowledged literary genre; that the publication is not without literary merit and could, divested of its undesirable aspects, be an acceptable medium of literary expression for, particularly, Black writers; that the threshold of undesirability is less easily crossed in the case of Blacks who do not have the same avenues of public protest as Whites; that poetic licence generally applies to publications of this nature; and, finally, that

the probable reader in South Africa would mainly include persons interested in the development of Black literature.

The committee found, however, that the factors mentioned do not outweigh the undesirable material present in this particular issue.

3. The undesirable material is mostly confined to unfair, one-sided and offensive portrayals of police actions and methods, calculated to evoke hatred and contempt of them. The Appeal Board has on several occasions pointed out that the police have been authorized by the State to maintain law and order, and that material calculated to bring them into contempt and to undermine their authority as a body is prejudicial to the safety of the State under *section 47 (2) (e)*.

4. Material which is particularly calculated to promote the undesirable results mentioned in the previous paragraph includes the following:

(a) The article *Awakening* by Amelia House (p. 8), whose address is given as Kentucky, USA. (It is not improbable that this may be a pseudonym for someone more closely connected to South Africa and, should this decision become the subject of appeal, the committee may call on the Appellant to identify this person more clearly. She (or he) is conversant with Afrikaans, as can be judged from the phrases 'kaffir,' 'geleerde Hotnot,' 'dronklap' and 'Hod jou bek, hotnot' in the article).

The undesirability of the article consists mainly in the scene in which the policeman indirectly encourages other arrested persons to urinate on Eric, a Black student; the scene where the 'good' Sergeant De Vos cannot force himself to protect Eric; the reference to the police shooting students in the back; the scenes of the brutal treatment of Dr. Jay and Eric; and the knife fight during the urinating incident.

(b) The poem *Tribute to Mapetha* by *Bafana Buthelezi/ Botswana* on *p. 49*. Two persons with that name are known— one a member of SASO and the other a member of the ANC. The committee has no conclusive proof that the writer of this poem is one of the two. Mapetla Mohapi who had been detained under the Terrorism Act, had been found hanged in his cell in the Kei Road jail in King William's Town. Unsubstantiated allegations that he had been killed by the police were subsequently made. The inquest magistrate found that Mohapi's death was due to anoxia and suffocation as a result of hanging, and was not brought about by any act of commission or omission by any living person. The poem appears to regard Mohapi as a revolutionary, and he is lauded as such. His blood supposedly would have nourished the Black Power fist after he had been 'murdered.' The people, as in Vietnam and Cuba, would also have been more powerful than the guns of Azania. ('Azania,' incidentally, is the PAC/Poqo term for South Africa). The poem is calculated to approve of subversive deeds; and to present Communist victories as laudable, as well as being a foretaste of what is to come in South Africa. The poet also accuses the police of murder. These factors taken together make the poem prejudicial to the safety of the State under *section 47 (2) (e)*.

The undesirability of these two poems makes the whole of the publication undesirable. An aggravating factor is that *Staffrider* is also offering a medium of expression for virulent attacks on South Africa's institutions by hostile persons living abroad.

5. Other poems or articles which contain undesirable matter under *section 47 (2) (e)* but which, on their own, could have been balanced by the favourable factors mentioned in par. 2, are the following: They are 'Why, Tumelo My Son?' on *p. 11* (Tumelo is found hanged in his cell. He had been beaten up by the police): 'Staffrider' on *p. 12*; 'Silence in Jail' on *p. 17* by Peter Horn); 'An African Woman' on *p. 36*; 'A Son of the First Generation' (a story of a transgression of the Immorality Act) (p. 24); and 'Notes on the Steps' on *p. 42*. Taken collectively, these poems and article add up to material which is definitely undesirable.

Mention should also be made of the sour attitude of Sheila Fugard in her poem 'The Voortrekkers' against the Afrikaners The latter should return to the countries of their origin lest the Blacks shoot them. Such racist attacks are of course most deplorable, but the committee believes that the average Afrikaner can absorb and adapt this particular piece of incentive coming from the indicated source (*p. 48*), and it does accordingly not fall within the meaning of *section 47 (2) (c) and (d).'*

Yours faithfully,
(SIGNED) DIRECTOR OF PUBLICATIONS

AN OPEN LETTER TO THE DIRECTOR OF PUBLICATIONS

Dear Sir,

Thank you for your letter giving us reasons for the committee's banning* of *Staffrider Vol. 2 No. 1*. Once again we have delayed an issue in order to publish your letter and our reply, since we regard this as an important dialogue which we are anxious to sustain in the hope that it may lead to something yet more important: the freedom and security of a debate within South Africa in which all may participate. It is our belief that art may prove to be the catalyst for such a debate, the chief topic of which would be the reconciliation of all South Africans within a society which would heal the bitterness presently felt —and so amply testified by black writers in particular.

We welcome the fullness of your letter: when you list the 'favourable factors' taken into consideration by the committee it is clear that a genuine inclination towards tolerance exists, on excellent grounds. The survival of *Staffrider* during 1978 (after banning and our exchange of views at that time) was already evidence of this, which is now confirmed. However we know that you will expect us, in the spirit of dialogue, to challenge your reasons with our own: here goes.

We feel that the brunt of your objection to Vol 2 No. 1 is carried in point four of your letter, which relates to *The Awakening* and *Tribute to Mapetla*. That this story and this poem have been singled out and pointedly described as "virulent attacks on South Africa's institutions by hostile persons living abroad' highlights, in our view, an absolutely central issue: is the debate in South Africa, in which art may lead the way, to exclude South Africans in exile? Whether Amelia House *is* Amelia House, whether Bafana Buthelezi is a member of SASO or the ANC (we are inviting them to write and tell us, if they wish to, in the pages of *Staffrider;* and asking Amelia, too, whether she regards your interest in whether she's male or female as an instance of sexism)—these, you may agree, are not the vital points.

What is really at stake is whether South Africans in exile (and, at the final count, will they be less South Africans for that?) are to be included in the internal debate if they wish to participate, or not? We must expect their contributions to be critical, but can we equate 'hostility' to what they perceive as the injustice of certain institutions and events, with hostility to their motherland itself?

We believe very strongly that the exclusion of exiled South Africans—of whatever political persuasion in our increasingly wide spectrum—from the practice of art in our country, and the ongoing debate on our future which art can stimulate, will be fatal to the already vulnerable hope of our writers and black countrymen for a peaceful future society enriched and nourished by a truly South African art. It is an 'aggravating factor' that to rule in favour of such an exclusion now will make it doubtful whether the response to any future invitation would be positive. It is an aggravating factor that, deprived of the significant exile voices, our internal art and dialogue through art will lack credibility. It must be acknowledged too that a high proportion of established black South African writers are exiles. We had hoped that in time their voices would be heard in *Staffrider;* your letter is, to say the least, a blow to that hope.

The other main point in your letter (para. 3) we answered in our open letter in reply to the banning of Vol. 1 No. 1. To this defence we still hold: the perception of the police as brutal by black writers, who are in rapport with the black community at large, is a sad fact of South African life which cannot be wished away. To disguise it by censorship can only exacerbate, not alleviate the problem. We accept that this perception must be deeply galling to some fine officers and men, but we believe that they would be the last to advocate sweeping the problem under the carpet.

Your objection (para. 5) to *Why Tumelo My Son?, Staffrider* (the poem), *An African Woman* and *Notes on the Steps* is answered above: in these cases your objection is based on the perceptions of the police displayed. We can only say that the story and three poems all convey fresh and genuine feelings: the impression they make is not one of cynical propaganda. They are clearly not intended as thorough and factual reports on reality: they are *perceptions* of reality, about which the reader can say, 'This is honestly felt' or 'I am not convinced that these feelings are genuine.' When honestly felt perceptions of reality are not permitted a hearing, we argue that the peaceful future of our society is endangered.

Your objection to *Silence in Jail* emphasizes the crucial nature of the representations we have made above on the question of exile writers: at present, indeed, their 'music crosses the border' only:

> 'on waves of ether
> through every crack
> between the heavily armed border posts.'

Your objection to *The Son of the First Generation* is particularly disheartening, since this is such a fresh and humane approach to the ancient theme of the Immorality Act. The controversial nature of the Act—the necessity of which has been disputed recently even by prominent members of the ruling party—surely makes it an obvious theme for fictional treatment.

Your closing remarks on Sheila Fugard's *The Voortrekkers*, in which you find a 'sour attitude' and a 'racist attack' seem to us to have mistaken the tone of her poem entirely. We are asking her to answer you in our next issue.

Yours sincerely,
THE PUBLISHERS

banned only for distribution

Glossary

Afrikaners—*Dutch descendents*

Coloured—*used to clasify people of mixed racial origin*

Daar's water—*There's the water*

dagga—*marijuana*

dronklap—*drunkard*

geleerde Hotnot—*educated "Coloured"*

Hotnot—*corruption of Hottentot; perjorative term for Khoikhoi indigenous people*

Hou jou bêk, Hotnot—*Shut up*

ja—*yes*

jong, kom—*boy, come*

Kaffir—*perjorative term for Black South African (equal nigger)*

kat—*cat*

Knobkieries—*carved walking sticks with knobs at one end; could serve as weapon*

konstabel—*constable*

maak nie saak nie—*it doesn't matter*

moet stil bly—*just keep quiet; don't talk*

mossie eier—*sparrow's egg*

sies—*exclamation of disgust; ugh!*

skollies (skolly, *singular*)—*members of street gangs*

stoep—*verandah*

Acknowledgements

We wish to thank the following journals and individuals for permission to reprint their work.

A Journey, *Tsetlo*.
A Luta Continua, Keorapetse Kgositsile.
A Piano Toccata by Baldassare Galuppi, *Censures and Salutes*.
A Poem, *Tsetlo*.
A Prayer for Africa from the Mouths of Babies, *Medu Art Ensemble Newsletter*.
All Hungers Pass Away, *Lonely Against the Light*.
Another Alexandra, *Tsetlo*.
At a Funeral, *A Simple Lust*.
Austin Moving Along Ballad, *GAR*.
Awakening, *Staffrider*.
Brief Thunder at Sharpeville, Nortje's Private Journals, David Bunn & Dennis Brutus.
Carnival at New Years, Julian deWette.
Chimid: A Memorial, Keorapetse Kgositsile.
Christmas 1976, Barbara J. Masekela.
Courtenay Rocks, Nortje's Private Journals, David Bunn & Dennis Brutus.
Creator, Julian deWette.
Dead Roots, *African Literature Today*.
Demon Exile, Barbara J. Masekela.
Dimbaza, *Black Voices Shout*.
Drink from My Empty Cup, *Black As I Am*.
ERA, *GAR*.
Exploration, Nortje's Private Journals, David Bunn & Dennis Brutus.
For My Unborn Child, Keorapetse Kgositsile.
Foreign Body, *Lonely Against the Night*.
Guerrilla, *South African Voices*.
Hanged, Dennis Brutus.
Heaven Is Not Closed, *Forced Landing*.
I share the pain of my black brother, *Cry Rage*.
I waited for you last night, *Black As I Am*.
In Memoriam, *BLAC*.
In the Black Gut, *BLAC*.
Isandhlwana Incarnate, Keorapetse Kgositsile.
It is night, James Matthews.
June 16 Year of the Spear, Keorapetse Kgositsile.

Biographies

Willie Adams
is a poet from Cape Town whose work has appeared in BLAC,
Staffrider, *and other publications.* (p. 28)

Dikeni Bayi
*is a South African writer from the Cape Province exiled in the
United States. Mr. Bayi's perceptive reviews of contemporary
South African literature have appeared in* GAR. (p. 88)

Dennis Brutus
*is a major literary figure in contemporary South African litera-
ture. His works include:* Sirens, Knuckles, and Boots; Letters To
Martha; Strains; China Poems; *and* Poems From Algiers. *His
works are collected in* A Simple Lust, *and* Stubborn Hope. *Cur-
rently a Professor in the English Department of Northwestern
University in Evanston, Illinois, Mr. Brutus is a relentless fighter
against the inhumane arrangement in his country known as
Apartheid. A forthcoming volume of his poetry,* Censures and
Salutes, *will be published in Nigeria.* (pp. 25, 51, 73, 74, 92,
93, 112, 138)

David Bunn
*is a young scholar from South Africa specializing in South
African Literature at Northwestern University. Mr. Bunn has
completed several inquiries on the journals of the late Arthur
Nortje.* (p. 116)

Austin Cloete
is a poet whose work appears in Black Voices Shout!, *an
anthology of work from the Black Consciousness Movement
which was banned in S.A.* (p. 80)

Julian deWette
is a poet who is living in exile in New York. (pp. 34, 64)

Christine Douts
is a poet whose work has appeared in Black Voices, Shout!,
GAR, *and other publications.* (p. 106)

Dumile Feni
*is a South African artist and sculptor living in exile in New
York City. He has had work exhibited at the United Nations,
the Museum of Modern Art, and various galleries* (pp. Front
cover, ii, 15, 39, 69, 85, 91, 99, 109, 115, 123).

Pascal Gwala
is a writer who has published one volume of poetry, Jol'inkomo, *with Ad Donker in Johannesburg; Mr. Gwala's work has also appeared in* Forced Landing, *an anthology by Raven Press, banned in S.A.* GAR *and* Black Voices, Shout! *have also published his work.* (p. 105)

Bessie Head
is a novelist from Pietermaritzburg whose major works are When Rain Clouds Gather *and* A Question of Power. Ms. *Head's work has appeared in a number of magazines and publications, including:* Transition, New African, Classic, Forced Landing, *and* More Modern African Stories. *She is exiled in Botswana.* (p. 41)

Amelia House
is both fiction writer and poet whose book reviews and essays have appeared in Presence Africain. *Her work has also appeared in* Staffrider. *She lives in Louisville, Kentucky.* (p. 54)

Baleka Kgositsile
is both wife and comrade of Keorapetse Kgositsile. Her poetry has appeared in Sechaba. *Both her life and her work are dedicated uncompromisingly to the liberation of South Africa.* (p. 100)

Keorapetse Kgositsile
is a major contemporary South African poet whose books include: My Name Is Afrika, For Melba, Spirits Unchained, The Present is a Dangerous Place to Live, Places and Bloodstains, *and* Heartprints. *Kgositisile's work has appeared in many magazines including:* Black World, Transition, Pan-African Journal, Sechaba, *and* Okike. *Currently, he resides in Dar es Salaam where he teaches at the University.* (pp. 20, 30, 52, 82, 86, 96, 136, 144)

Bheki Langa
is a South African poet in exile, dedicated to returning South Africa to the hands of its people. (p. 102)

Mandlenkosi Langa
Mandlenkosi Langa's work has appeared in MEDU Art Ensemble Newsletter,; *he has been exiled in Botswana.* (p. 113)

Ilva McKay
Ilva McKay's work has appeared in: Black Voices, Shout!, BLAC, *and* Sechaba. *She now lives in exile.* (p. 107)

Zindzi Mandela
*is the daughter of Nelson Mandela, President of the African
National Congress who is now serving time in the
infamous Robben Island prison as a political prisoner. Zindzi
Mandela is co-author of* black as i am *along with the photog-
rapher Peter Mugubane; her work has appeared in* Sechaba. *She
lives in South Africa.* (pp. 17, 27, 79)

Barbara Masakela
*has lived in the United States for the last 15 years. Except for
her brother, her family still resides in South Africa. She studied
Zulu language and literature at Roma College, Lesotho. Cur-
rently she teaches Black and Women's literature at Rutgers
University.* (pp. 65, 66, 67, 68, 84, 90)

Victor Matlou
*is a very gifted poet living in exile in Africa and working to
return South Africa to all the people.* (p. 128)

James Matthews
*is a veteran fighter for the rights of his people. He has pub-
lished many young Black South African writers in* BLAC *and*
Black Voices, Shout! *which he edited. His short stories have
been widely anthologized and his work appears in* Forced
Landing. *Mr. Matthews is a grand man who ceaselessly criti-
cizes the inhumane policies of the government sponsoring
Apartheid. He is a committed writer.* (pp. 40, 81, 94)

Arthur Nortje
*Arthur Nortje was born in Port Elizabeth, South Africa and was
in exile in London at the time of his tragic death in 1970. His
volumes of poetry are:* Lonely Against the Light *and* Dead
Roots. *His work has appeared in* MEDU Art Ensemble News-
letter, African Literature Today, The Greenfield Review, Black
Orpheus, *and* Modern Poetry From Africa. *Fifteen of Mr.
Nortje's unpublished poems have been recently discovered in
his Oxford Journal where his ideas about himself and his work
are recorded. His untimely death represents a major loss.*
(pp. 18, 22, 24, 49, 70, 95, 117, 118, 119, 120, 121, 122)

Matime Papane
Matime Papane's poetry appears in Staffrider. (p. 35)

Essop Patel
*is an Indian writer living in the ghettoes of South Africa; his
work has appeared in* Staffrider. (p. 36)

Cosmo Pieterse
*is a tenured professor in the English Department in Athens,
Ohio. He has edited several volumes of poetry and drama,
including* Seven South African Poets. Echoes and Choruses *is a
collection of Mr. Pieterse's poetry.* (pp. 110, 127)

Sterling Plumpp
*is an Assistant Professor in the Black Studies Program, Univer-
sity of Illinois at Chicago Circle. His books include* Portable
Soul; Half Black, Half Blacker; Steps to Break the Circle;
Clinton; Common Hands; The Mojo Hands Call I Must Go
(forthcoming from Thunder's Mouth Press); and Black Rituals,
a collection of prose pertaining to Black culture.

Sidney Sepamla
lives in South Africa; his published works include: Hurry Up
To It, The Soweto I Love, *and* The Blues Is You In Me. *His
work is widely anthologized.* (pp. 32, 37, 71)

Jaki Seroke
resides in South Africa and his poems have appeared in
Staffrider. (p. 78)

Mongane Serote
*is the recipient of a MFA from Columbia University in New
York; his published volumes of poetry include:* Yahnal'inkomo,
Tsetlo, No Baby Must Weep, *and* Behold Mama, Flowers. *He
is currently exiled in Botswana. His work is widely anthologized.*
(pp. 16, 72, 75, 104, 111, 124)